Paradox in Chesterton

Paradox in Chesterton

By HUGH KENNER

Introduction by Herbert Marshall McLuhan

New York
SHEED & WARD
1947

Manufactured in the United States of America
by The Haddon Craftsmen, Inc.

To My Mother

My thanks are due to several friends who have read, criticized, and corrected the manuscript; in particular to the Rev. L. K. Shook, C.S.B., of St. Michael's College, University of Toronto, and to the Rev. Gerald B. Phelan, formerly of the Pontifical Institute of Mediaeval Studies, Toronto. The aid and encouragement of Dr. Herbert Marshall McLuhan has gone far beyond the preparation of the Introduction.

—W. H. K.

ACKNOWLEDGMENTS

We are grateful to the following publishers for their kind permission to quote from these books: Dodd, Mead & Co.: *Alarms and Discursions, Collected Poems, The Everlasting Man, Heretics, Irish Impressions, The Napoleon of Notting Hill, Orthodoxy, Tremendous Trifles, The Uses of Diversity,* by Gilbert K. Chesterton; *G. K. Chesterton, A Criticism,* by Cecil Chesterton; E. P. Dutton & Co., Inc.: *William Blake,* by G. K. Chesterton.

CONTENTS

CHAPTER   PAGE

Introduction xi

I. Preliminary 1

II. Paradox and Its Necessity 12

III. The Idea of Analogy 24

IV. The Word 40

V. The World 58

VI. The Word and the World 103

Notes 143

INTRODUCTION

TO-DAY THE Chesterton public remains very much the public which read his books as they appeared. And for these readers he inevitably represents a variety of literary attitudes and manners which have begun to "date" in a way which bars many younger readers from approaching him. So that, for example, even in Catholic colleges books by Chesterton are not commonly on the reading-lists, nor do many of the present crop of students read anything more by him than an occasional "Father Brown."

The present book strikes out a line of radical evaluation which should do much to save Chesterton from this growing indifference. For in presenting him as a master of analogical perception and argument, Mr. Kenner at once divorces the Toby-jug Chesterton of a particular literary epoch from the central and important Chesterton who had an unwavering and metaphysical intuition of being. The specific contemporary relevance of Chesterton is this, that his metaphysical intuition of being was always in the service of the search for moral and political order in the current chaos. He was a Thomist by connaturality with being, not by study of St. Thomas. And unlike the neo-Thomists his unfailing sense of the relevance of the analogy of being directed his intellectual gaze not to the schoolmen but to the heart of the chaos of our time.

The point of the comparison may be made plain in this way. St. Thomas carried on his systematic speculation in the thirteenth century. Behind that century there lay fifteen centuries of encyclopaedic irrationalism. From the decline of the briefly-achieved Greek order in politics and morals the West was dominated not by rationalism but by psychologism. That is, the cosmologies which were held up for the contemplation of men, whether Stoic or Epicurean, Divine Logos or concourse of atoms, were not philosophies but psychologies. They were strategies of a moral kind evolved as a practical means of bearing up against the universal confusion.

When the Church Fathers adapted the neo-Platonic and Stoic concept of the Logos to Christian Revelation, they committed the Church to many centuries of symbolism and allegory. The result was that for a very long time the outer world was seen as a net-work of analogies which richly exemplified and sustained the psychological and moral structure of man's inner world. Both inner and outer worlds were mirrors in which to contemplate the Divine Wisdom. Society, national and international, grew up once more. And it was an organic and closely-knit society in which the individual enjoyed a very high degree of psychological if not physical security, because of the universal acceptance of the moral and social implications of the Divine order mirrored simultaneously in physical nature, human nature, and political organization. Shakespeare is never more mediaeval than when he is stating this view of man and society. It is one of his favorite themes, as when his Ulysses says

The heavens themselves, the planets and this centre
Observe degree, priority, and place,
Insisture, course, proportion, season, form,
Office and custom in all line of order.

.... O! When degree is shak'd,
Which is the ladder to all high designs,
The enterprise is sick. How could communities,
Degrees in schools, and brotherhood in cities,
Peaceful commerce from dividable shores,
The primogeniture and due of birth,
Prerogative of age, crowns, sceptres, laurels,
But by degree, stand in authentic place?
Take but degree away, untune that string, ...
Then everything includes itself in power,
Power into will, will into appetite;
And appetite, an universal wolf,
So doubly seconded with will and power,
Must make perforce an universal prey
And last eat up itself.

That is already a rather rationalistic and mechanical formulation, because Shakespeare wrote when this great symbolic and psychological synthesis was really destroyed. But in the thirteenth century St. Thomas was situated in the midst of a world in which psychological and symbolic awareness of order was almost the only awareness. His great rational synthesis represented a maximum degree of abstraction and withdrawal from that psychological plane of symbolic perception. But it should be emphasized that St. Thomas never rejected that psychological order. He took it for granted. He was sustained and nourished by it. And he never questioned or denied its value. In fact, the degree and scope of his rational synthesis is inconceivable without it.

But St. Thomas was followed by a host of rationalizers who were not so much nourished by the great symbolic cultural unity of the previous centuries as irritated by some contemporary rationalizer. St. Thomas had restored the anti-symbolic Aristotle to his proper role in systematic thought. But for every schoolman who understood the due relation between Aristotle and Plato or between Aristotle and the Church Fathers there were hundreds of noisy disputants who had their way to make in the world. By the early seventeenth century Descartes could rally enthusiastic support for the proposition that since no philosopher had ever been convinced by the dialectical or metaphysical proofs of other philosophers for the truth of anything, therefore the time had come to introduce a kind of proof which all men could accept—namely, mathematical proof.

What Descartes really did was to make explicit the fact which had been prepared by centuries of decadent scholastic rationalism: the fact that a complete divorce had been achieved between abstract intellectual and specifically psychological order. Henceforth men would seek intellectually only for the kind of order they could readily achieve by rationalistic means: a mathematical and mechanistic order which precludes a human and psychological order. Ethics and politics were abandoned as much as metaphysics. But both society and philosophy were in a state of great confusion by the time this desperate strategy was adopted.

Since the time of Descartes the strategy has been followed consistently. A high degree of abstract mechanical order has been achieved. Great discoveries of a potentially benign sort have been made. And human moral, psychological, and political chaos has steadily developed, with its concurrent crop of fear and anger and hate. The rational efforts of men have been wholly diverted from the ordering of appetite and emotion, so that any effort to introduce or to discover order in man's psychological life has been left entirely to the artist. Whereas the mediaeval artist was a relatively anonymous person whose function was not to discover order but to represent an already achieved psychological unity, the modern artist is regarded as a pioneer:

> his sail-broad vans
> He spreads for flight, and in the surging smoke
> Uplifted spurns the ground; thence many a league
> As in a cloudy chair ascending rides
> Audacious.

As the contemporary artist attempts to chart the psychological chaos created in the heart of man by a mechanistic society his activity is scanned with the utmost concern. A Blake, a Wordsworth, a Baudelaire, a Rimbaud, a Picasso, or a Rouault is regarded as a major source of hope and discovery. The disproportionate burden placed on the artist is the measure of the failure of the philosophy.

The point of the preceding diagnosis is this: that whereas St. Thomas was a great abstract synthesizer facing a unified psychological world, the modern Thomist has an abstract synthesis of human knowledge with which to face a psychological chaos. Who then is the true Thomist? The man who contemplates an already achieved intellectual synthesis, or the man who, sustained by that synthesis, plunges into the heart of the chaos? I say "sustained", not guided by, that synthesis; because the Catholic Thomist does not know the answers to contemporary problems in social and political ethics. He knows only when a particular line of action is promising and analogically consistent, whether it will tend to support a valid solution, and whether it is in conformity with reason and being. But he is the reverse of fecund in such proposals.

Let us remember that St. Thomas was sustained by a great psychological and social order in an age of dialectical confusion. We can be similarly sustained and nourished in an organic way by his speculative synthesis while we face the problem of creating a practical moral and social order. The main problem for Thomists to-day, therefore, is not speculation but action. And this necessarily means an action which co-operates in multiple ways with the numerous hopeful features of the contemporary world.

To take an example. Catholics have failed to understand or utilize Vico. Vico's great discovery of a psychological method for interpreting historical periods and cultural patterns is rooted in his perception that the condition of man is never the same but his nature is unchanging. For two centuries the Viconian method has been used by those who denied the rational form of man and who had only the desire to destroy rather than to perfect social order. Spengler finally perverted it to the support of paranoiac rationalism. On the other hand, the first strikingly valid use of the Viconian method occurs in Gilson's *Unity of Philosophical Experience*. Vico was not a Thomist, and so he has been abandoned to the sceptics; but he invented an instrument of historical and cultural analysis of the utmost use for the discovery of psychological and moral unity in the practical order: something which St. Thomas was not interested in because such unity did, by and large, exist in his world.

Another example. The Catholic teaching of philosophy and the arts tends to be catechetical. It seeks precisely that Cartesian pseudo-certitude which it officially deplores, and divorces itself from the complex life of philosophy and the arts. This is only to say that the Catholic colleges are just like non-Catholic colleges: reflections of a mechanized world. The genuine critical discoveries, on the other hand, made by T. S. Eliot and F. R. Leavis, about how to train, simultaneously, esthetic and moral perceptions in acts of unified awareness and judgment: these major discoveries are ignored by Catholic educators. Rather in the rationalistic and dialectical patterns of Buchanan and Adler they imagine that there is some Thomistic residue which is to be trusted.

That is where Chesterton comes in. His unfailing sense of relevance and of the location of the heart of the contemporary chaos carried him at all times to attack the problem of morals and psychology. He was always in the practical order. It is important, therefore, that a Chesterton anthology should be made along the lines indicated by Mr. Kenner. Not an anthology which preserves the Victorian flavor of his journalism by extensive quotation, but one of short excerpts which would permit the reader to feel Chesterton's powerful intrusion into every kind of confused moral and psychological issue of our time. For he seems never to have reached any position by dialectic or doctrine, but to have enjoyed a kind of connaturality with every kind of reasonableness.

So very impressive is this metaphysical side of Chesterton that it is always embarrassing to encounter the Chesterton fan who is keen about *The Ballad of the White Horse* or the hyperbolic descriptive parts of Chesterton's prose. In fact, it might be the kindest possible service to the essential Chesterton to decry all that part of him which derives so obviously from his time. Thus it is absurd to value Chesterton for that large and unassimilated heritage he got from William Morris—the big, epic dramaturgic gestures, riotous colour, mediaeval trappings, ballad themes and banal rhythms. Morris manages these things better than Chesterton ever did: and nobody wants to preserve William Morris.

There is also a lot of irrelevant pre-Raphaelite rhetoric in Chesterton. From Rosetti came those pale auburn-haired beauties who invariably haunt his stories. The tiresome alliteration is from Swinburne. From Edward Lear came the vein of anarchic nursery wisdom which served the Victorians as a strategy for keeping sane. By acting insane in a childish way, a kind of temporary equilibrium was maintained: but it was also an evasion of that world of adult horror into which Baudelaire gazed with intense suffering and humility. For the Victorians the nursery was the only tap-root connecting them with psychological reality. But for Chesterton the rhetoric and dimensions of childhood had also their true Christian vigor and scope. He was never tempted into the *cul-de-sac* in which the *faux-naïf* of the Christopher Robin variety invariably winds up.

Nevertheless, there is in Chesterton a considerable aroma of the desperate jauntiness and pseudo-energy of the world of Stevensonian romance: enough to make it desirable to give back to Stevenson the things that are Stevenson's rather than to try to make this dubious adolescent rhetoric appear to be of equal value with Chesterton's metaphysical intuition of being. From Stevenson's master Henley, Chesterton adopted the note of professional heartiness—a journalist's strategy for debunking the esthetish despair of the eighties and nineties. It has led to Kipling and Bulldog Drummond. Henley fathered the optimistic reaction to the intellectual langour of the later Victorians, and *Wine, Water and Song* is typical of Chesterton's sympathy with that sort of lugubriously self-conscious jollity. But just how unessential it was to him is plain from the fact that Chesterton really was happy. Henley and Kipling never were.

One Victorian feature of Chesterton's which is more closely allied to his real strength he got from Oscar Wilde: rhetorical paradox and epigram. Pater's *Marius the Epicurean* awoke to "that poetic and, as it were, moral significance which surely belongs to all the means of daily life, could we but break through the veil of our familiarity with things by no means vulgar in themselves." Wilde made much of this basic paradox in his life and art, as when in *The Decay of Lying* he proved that social and artificial things are more exciting than the "nature" of the romantic poets, and that "Life imitates Art far more than Art imitates Life."

The way in which Whitman and Browning and others appear in Chesterton is even more obvious. But the conclusion which it seems necessary to draw from these Victorian aspects of Chesterton is simply that he was not sufficiently interested in them to make a genuinely personal fusion of them. Had they been necessary to his primary awareness of things, he would have been obsessively limited by them in that drastic way in which a Stevenson or a Pater is limited and "dated."

In a word, Chesterton was not a poet. The superstition that he was is based on the vaguely uplifting connotations of "the poetic" prevalent until recently. He was a metaphysical moralist. Thus he had no difficulty in imagining what sort of psychological pressures would occur in the mind of a fourth-century Egyptian, or a Highland clansman, or a modern Californian, popping himself inside of them and seeing with their eyes in the way that makes Father Brown unique among detectives. But he was not engaged in rendering his own age in terms of such varied experience, as the artist typically is. The artist offers us not a system but a world. An inner world is explored and developed and then projected as an object. But that was never Chesterton's way. "All my mental doors open outwards into a world I have not made," he said in a basic formulation. And this distinction must always remain between the artist who is engaged in making a world and the metaphysician who is occupied in contemplating a world. It should also relieve the minds of those who from a sense of loyalty to Chesterton's philosophical power have felt obliged to defend his rhetoric and his verses as well.

It is time to abandon the literary and journalistic Chesterton to such critical fate as may await him from future appraisers. And it is also time to see him freed from the accidental accretions of ephemeral literary mannerisms. That means to see him as a master of analogical perception and argument who never failed to focus a high degree of moral wisdom on the most confused issues of our age.

—HERBERT MARSHALL MC LUHAN.

Paradox in Chesterton

I: PRELIMINARY

CHESTERTON IS not so much great because of his published achievement as great because he is right. His achievement deserves a homage less indiscriminate than it has yet been accorded, and that is part of my business in this book; but I do more than praise what he wrote: I praise what he knew. He cannot be praised too highly so long as praise is confined to what is praiseworthy. His especial gift was his metaphysical intuition of being; his especial triumph was his exploitation of paradox to embody that intuition.

He is plainly not a great literary artist. It would be folly, for example, to rank him with so disciplined a craftsman as T. S. Eliot. He is a great moral philosopher, and like his Master, a great physician of souls and minds. But Chesterton the writer scarcely left a page that is not (as he would have cheerfully admitted) in some way botched or disfigured: nor is the deficiency that vitiates the bulk of his poetry and fiction merely technical. His perceptions were metaphysical rather than aesthetic: they never fathered creative fusion. One might almost say that they were too comprehensive and vivid to be fused.

That is as far as blame need go. If Chesterton is not, like Eliot in his poetry, creative, he is never, like Eliot in his later essays, irresponsible. If he cannot practice art in its major sense, as creation, he practices it constantly in its broader sense, as making; and what he makes is never trivial: it is always geared to his extraordinary metaphysical perception. Here, in this less intense form of aesthetic activity, if he is not great he is sane. Art consists first in knowing and then in making. Chesterton knew, and knew how to make; he merely did not polish what he made.

I propose to justify paradox as Chesterton used it, as a means to truth and as a means to art, understanding by art all making. I propose to imply how far the Edwardian decay of art and thought is traceable to the denial of paradox; and to indicate how the modern intellectual recovery is sound exactly in proportion as it recaptures principles which Chesterton almost alone among his contemporaries saw with clarity and confidence.

That the poet must conquer the dictionary and the thinker overmaster the syllogism is a principal critical discovery of an age whose concern has been to revolutionize thought without thinking and to revitalize art without producing beautiful things.

Art and thought have for forty years been rediscovering their proper dramatic tension between opposites: poetry disdaining the idiot herding proclivities of words to wrestle, as it must, a reconciliation between words and things; thought grappling both with things and with itself, fighting its own facile lapses away from reality.

The force of these twin discoveries is attested by the loneliness and misunderstanding that have beset the discoverers. Eliot is damned as a dilettante and Joyce, once hailed as a naturalist, is decried as an obscurantist by men who, misunderstanding the high tradition they have recovered, praise Shakespeare for the wrong reasons and hence do not praise his modern disciples at all. Maritain, bringing life to scholastic logic, is similarly slighted by sceptics who fancy that the end of philosophy is not knowledge but entertainment and who know his master St. Thomas (when they know him at all) rather as a quaintly encyclopaedic mediaeval speculator than as a lover of wisdom striving to set down the real nature of things.

This mistaking of the auxiliary for the essential has operated to the grave disservice of Gilbert Chesterton. Having participated for forty years in the rediscovery of thought, he is apologized for as an inspired idiot; having, with a welcome Elizabethan exuberance, recaptured that wonder before words which unites with a parallel wonder before things to issue in art, he is alternately labelled a funny fellow and a propagandist. On both counts academic criticism runs true to form. Chesterton, however, has not altogether followed his companions in art and thought into popular oblivion: the oblivion, for example, that unfairly overwhelms his great friend Belloc. He is tolerated and even loved where the others are rebuffed and discarded, because he was in himself lovable and in his art paradoxical. His paradoxes have tickled where they should have stung. There is no more irritating example of the critical habit of being nearly right.

The heart of Chesterton's thinking and writing is his perception and use of paradox; yet because, as Belloc observed, it satisfies men for the wrong reason, it has been a principal hindrance to his rapid acceptance as an important thinker and writer. What appears to be superficial playing is really an intense plumbing among the mysterious roots of being and language; but in a sort of exhausted relief that this profound but disturbing visionary need not be read profoundly, his critics have neglected the intensity and enjoyed only the play.

A little reflection will show, however, that the paradoxes of Chesterton are both a ready introduction and a useful key to those new awarenesses which offer hope of restoring civilization. For to perceive paradox is to escape the error of the thinker whose thought leads him away from reality, and to use paradox is to avoid the sin of the poet whose words file flabbily, like a procession of sheep, ever away and away from human tensions.

Chesterton must be taken seriously because paradox must be taken seriously, both as a tool of expression and as an ingredient of reality. He was not, as he has been so readily called, a maker of paradoxes. I propose to show that he did not make them, but saw them: his caprice was thrust upon him. Nor was it even caprice. From the critical tradition that sees something contemptible even in a good paradox, I appeal to an older tradition which finds paradox in the deepest mysteries and is driven to paradoxical language in the simplest statements of what it sees. Mr. Eliot plainly does homage to this tradition in his revival of "metaphysical" poetry; and a given paragraph of vintage Chesterton is not unlike a metaphysical poem. Chesterton wrote as he did because he saw, and not because he wanted to make a stir; and he saw the world as madly as he did because his eyes were especially open, and not because his mind was especially perverse, or especially perverted. When late in life he came to grips with systematic philosophy, he was able to produce without apparent effort[1] a profound study of St. Thomas Aquinas, because St. Thomas expounded in an or-

derly and systematic fashion what Gilbert Chesterton
had been seeing and saying all his life.

There would be no difficulty in showing that
Chesterton was in sympathy with St. Thomas long
before he had presumably even heard of him. Neither
Thomism nor anything else was a perception of his
later life, because all his thought rests on a single
lifelong perception of being that is deepened but
never shifted: the same is true of the thought of St.
Thomas. And Chesterton was from the very beginning a philosophical realist. His cardinal metaphysical principle was "to say very emphatically (with
a blow on the table), 'There *is* an Is'."[2] " 'Material-
ists,' " he makes Gabriel Gale say in another passage,
" 'are all right; they are at least near enough to
heaven to accept the earth and not imagine they
made it. The dreadful doubts are not the doubts of
the materialist. The dreadful doubts, the deadly and
damnable doubts, are the doubts of the idealist.' "[3]

Chesterton, then, began at the Thomistic starting-
point, which is being and not thought. Hence I
have felt safe in using throughout this book such
terms as "Being," "Reality," "Analogy," and
"Truth," in their Thomistic sense, confident that
in that strict sense they really do express what Chesterton meant. St. Thomas lends himself better than
Chesterton to systematic treatment; not because
Chesterton was an unsystematic thinker, but because

he was a wildly unsystematic and digressive writer. I have therefore begun with the Thomistic doctrine of analogy, because the essential preliminary ideas must be put in some sort of arrangement, and St. Thomas and his commentators have arranged them better than anyone else.

The progression within this book is from paradox in general to paradox in Chesterton. The next two chapters discuss, respectively, the necessity of paradox as an ingredient in things and in art, and its secure philosophical roots in the Aquinatian principle of analogy. The remaining three chapters classify the paradoxes of Chesterton for separate investigation: paradox in words, a rhetorical strategy; paradox in things, a metaphysical perception; and paradox in that union of words and things which is literary art.

In the Christian Fathers, sundry theologians, and in as diverse an array of poets as Donne, Traherne, Crashaw, Blake, and James Joyce, one may find analogues for Chesterton's paradoxes at every level. Paradox is not a decadent invention but a rooted tradition, especially a Christian tradition; it is rooted in the world-stuff which a contemplative sees, and Chesterton was first of all a contemplative. At twenty-two he scribbled in his Notebook, under the title, "The Grace of Our Lord Jesus Christ," what must have been one of the first of his paradoxes:

I live in an age of varied powers and knowledge,
Of steam, science, democracy, journalism, art;
But when my love rises like a sea,
I have to go back to an obscure tribe and a slain man
To formulate a blessing.[4]

And in the full tide of maturity his language grapples
with the same overwhelming vision of slain Divinity:

When from the deeps a dying God astounded
Angels and devils who do all but die . . ."[5]

It is significant both of the fundamental seriousness
of Chesterton's intention and of his orientation
within the long tradition of Christian paradox, that
these two paradoxes, representative of his first and
his last, spring from the contemplation of the same
event. There is even a sense in which, as we shall see,
the majority of his multitudinous demonstrations
of the paradoxical are traceable to his perception of
that root paradox at the heart of the cosmos: the
God who died. Paradox, intrinsic in language, in
thought, and in reality, comes to the surface so much
in Chesterton only because he is especially conscious
of intrinsic things—that is, of ultimate things.

A man conscious of ultimate things presents difficulties in the peculiar compactness of his thinking
and writing: so much so that when the elements of
his vision are once grasped, one may use almost any
stray citation to illustrate any part of it. Such a
remark as "Man cannot love mortal things; he can

only love immortal things for an instant,"[6] is a verbal paradox, a clear-cut illustration of a word used analogically (the word "love"), a metaphysical statement involving a whole philosophy of God and the universe, and (in its proper place in *Heretics*) the climax of a refutation of hedonism embedded in an essay urging the right use of wine. There is a penultimate stage of disillusion in the study of Chesterton wherein he seems merely to be saying the same thing over and over again; the ultimate stage is to realize that he says it so often because it can never really be said; in fact, because there is nothing else to say. Where he has to some extent failed, as all art must fail, this book cannot attempt to succeed; hence the extent to which the following pages repeat and anticipate one another, so as to prevent what is really in Chesterton an immediate vision from looking as though it were, or were intended to be, a connected argument.

There remains one radical misconception of Chesterton which eludes my general scheme, and may well be disposed of here. It is the notion that Chesterton is paradoxical merely because he is perversely in opposition; that his paradoxes consist chiefly in contradictions of what people around him are saying, for the mere sake of contradiction.[7]

It is manifest that he does so contradict: but he does not die with the causes he refutes. He is not essentially the child of his times, no matter what quantity of his temporary journalism has faded. That much is evident in the fact that he does not merely react to contemporary confusions, but cuts through them. In assessing a mind whose immediate mark is perpetual opposition to his surroundings, perpetual baiting of the great in his age, and perpetual controversy with the popular champions, one must never forget that such opposition is by nature dual: there are minds like knives, and minds like buffers. The difficulty is that they are both described as minds in opposition. Bernard Shaw really is a child of the twentieth century, or rather of the late nineteenth, however much he may kick against its institutions, because his dislike of one popular prejudice merely presupposes a contrary one. He is logical rather than penetrating. The essence of Bernard Shaw, of your typical clever reactionary, is to be always evident because always in motion, but always in motion because always on the rebound. Shaw is the mirror of the social structure he abominates, because in reversing it he reflects it unchanged. His fame would be inconceivable without it, as a mirror is meaningless with nothing to reflect. Chesterton on the contrary, for all his borrowed fin-de-siècle trappings, would be in any age essentially what he is now: a wide-eyed child before facts, who does not trouble himself with the age except when the age denies the facts which he patently sees: as, unfortunately, it does all the time. He is not essentially a combatant; he is essentially a contemplative. It is a judgment on an altogether unsympathetic age that it so frequently forced him into combat, and so cost him the combatant's exhaustion of spiritual force that might have been more positively expended. Conversely, the dwellers of so ugly a time have been fortunate in having among them so potent a contemplative to combat it.

II: PARADOX AND ITS NECESSITY

THE SOMBRE, often inarticulate, wisdom of Hilaire Belloc, which has left as a final monument to both men a study of Gilbert Chesterton fragmentary and exasperating but unique in perception, depth, and right proportions, has in a phrase near the start of that work put the critical rabble in their place: "the half-educated and uncultured, who are of the stuff by which modern opinion is ruled, use of him the term 'paradoxical.' "[1]

Nothing is more suggestive about Chesterton's use of paradox than the fact that Belloc barely noticed it. Paradox was not, in his view, the touchstone of the Chestertonian method; to be obsessed by the paradoxes in Chesterton, Belloc implies, is to understand him imperfectly. For it seemed perfectly natural to Belloc, as he surveyed the achievement of his friend, that when thought by its force or complexity defied language, language should break.

It is fair to say, however, that most critics, and those not only "the half-educated and uncultured," have called Chesterton a maker of paradoxes. Here, as usual, popular surveys of literature furnish a useful index of the state of enlightened opinion. Thus Ifor Evans speaks of him "forcing prose into new effects, as if he were using his style as an advertisement for his thought. He seems like a poet corrupted in an age of advertisement."[2] Cazamian says that he "jingles noisily the bells of a paradoxical invention."[3] A reviewer of his first volume of essays remarked that "Paradox ought to be used like onions to season the salad. Mr. Chesterton's salad is all onions. Paradox has been defined as 'truth standing on her head to attract attention.' Mr. Chesterton makes truth cut her throat to attract attention."[4] More picturesque is Oliver Herford's impish account of the Chestertonian method:

> When plain folks such as you and I
> See the sun sinking in the sky,
> We think it is the setting sun:
> But Mr. Gilbert Chesterton
> Is not so easily misled;
> He calmly stands upon his head,
> And upside down obtains a new
> And Chestertonian point of view.
> Observing thus how from his toes
> The sun creeps closer to his nose
> He cries in wonder and delight
> How fine the sunrise is tonight![5]

Of more alarming implications, finally, is the comment of one Dr. Horace T. Bridges, who found in Chesterton, after debating with him, "a certain intellectual recklessness that made him indifferent to truth and reality . . . fundamentally—perhaps I should say subconsciously—he was a thoroughgoing sceptic and acted upon the principle that, since we cannot really be positive about anything we had better believe what it pleases us to believe."[6]

Chesterton himself never acceded to the charge of paradox-mongering, even as a means of making jokes; and on at least one occasion repudiated it with uncommon warmth.[7] In *Orthodoxy* he goes further:

Mere light sophistry is the thing that I happen to despise most of all things, and it is perhaps a wholesome fact that this is the thing of which I am most generally accused. I know nothing so contemptible as a mere paradox; a mere ingenious defense of the indefensible. If it were true (as has been said) that Mr. Bernard Shaw lived upon paradox, then he ought to be a mere common millionaire; for a man of his mental activity could invent a sophistry every six minutes. It is as easy as lying; because it is lying.[8]

Yet we find him continually and explicitly urging paradox on his readers without apology. "The tradition of Christianity," he writes in *Heretics*, ". . . rests on two or three paradoxes or mysteries which can easily be impugned in argument and as easily justified in real life;"[9] and the necessity of likeness as a basis of difference he calls "The first and simplest of the paradoxes that sit by the springs of truth."[10]

The point is that the paradoxes sit by the springs

of truth and not merely at the well-head of the Chestertonian humour; if, as he shows, you put the simplest truths in the simplest language, that language will seem to be contradicting itself, because of something inherently irreconcilable in the truths.

One of them, for instance, is the paradox of hope or faith—that the more hopeless is the situation, the more hopeful must be the man. . . . Another is the paradox of charity or chivalry that the weaker a thing is the more it should be respected, that the more indefensible a thing is the more it should appeal to us for a certain kind of defense.[11]

The truth is that there is good and bad paradox, just as there is good and bad art, just as there are shut and open eyes. Chesterton used paradox safely because he was first a contemplative and second an artist; first he saw, and then he made. Those who have made bad paradoxes, and dragged paradoxy into such disrepute thereby as to deprive Chesterton of half his proper audience, have spoken first, and not seen at all.

What good and bad paradoxes possess in common is the shock derived from contradiction: paradox *is* contradiction, explicit or implied.

Of his good paradoxes, it may be said in general that the implied kind have generally as their object the persuasion of the reader, and the explicit, the praise of God. To make an initial division in this way is to distinguish Chesterton the journalist from Chesterton the metaphysician. When he writes that "the hands that had made the sun and stars were too small to reach the huge heads of the cattle,"[12] he is in the tradition of Christian paradox that sustains, for example, the Nativity sermons of Bishop Andrewes: "I add yet farther; what flesh? The flesh of an infant. What, *verbum infans,* the Word an infant? The Word, and not able to speak a word? How evil agreeth this!"[13] When, on the other hand, he writes, "What ruins mankind is the ignorance of the expert,"[14] he is contradicting not himself but his reader, in language that would carry conviction like an arrow if the reader had not previously acquired different ideas. Where the reader got those ideas, and why he holds them, forms part of Chesterton's business; but his principal task is to rid him of those ideas, less by persuasion than by explosion.

There is, then, a metaphysical use of paradox that answers to the complexity of being, especially the Supreme Being, and a rhetorical use that answers merely to the complexity of human folly. The latter is essentially verbal, and obtains its effect through the juxtaposition of unlikely words, as in G.K.'s reference to Companionate Marriage, "So-called because the people involved are not married and will very rapidly cease to be companions."[15] The former is essentially metaphysical, because the intrinsic contradiction is not in the words but in the things. To escape metaphysical paradox does not lie within the will of the writer; verbal paradox he can achieve or abolish at will by the substitution of terms. He can get around the jingle and jugglery of the epigram about Companionate Marriage by simply calling it adultery; though that would lose the point of a trenchant satire on euphemism. But he cannot get around the mystery of the Trinity no matter how he tries; except by the deceptive dodge of refusing to think or talk about it at all.

The object of verbal paradox, then, is persuasion, and its principle is the inadequacy of words to thoughts, unless they be very carefully chosen words. But the principle of metaphysical paradox is something inherently intractable in being itself; in the Thing. Its immediate object is exegesis: its ultimate object is praise, awakened by wonder. Paradox springs in general from inadequacy, from the rents in linguistic and logical clothing; paradoxy might be called the science of gaps.

A third kind of paradox is discoverable in Chesterton, which depends upon the processes of art. The literary artist moves directly from things to words, and consummates their marriage; such logical difficulties as may entangle his mind in the process he keeps to himself. In marrying the word and the world, however, he creates what is in effect a third kind of paradox, the aesthetic: a resolution of the tensions within things and the tensions within language into a third kind of tension from which art takes its vitality. So that while an individual example may prove virtually impossible to classify, the paradoxes of Chesterton are in general verbal, metaphysical, and aesthetic, turning severally upon the Word, the World, and that union of the Word and the World which is Art.

Hence it is essential to the proper appreciation of Gilbert Chesterton to realize that paradox is not an extraordinary adornment of writing and speech, but rather almost their normal form. All humour rests on paradox, because every good joke is capped by the unexpected. The surprise ending is used or misused throughout literature: and it is a paradoxical ending. There is a sort of metaphysical paradox in the banishing of Falstaff, an act unexpected but implicit in the characters and in the nature of kingship. There is certainly a most mechanical form of rhetorical paradox in the common detective-story which manoeuvres the reader into passivity and proceeds to spring on him astonishing tidings of crimes performed by the harmless old aunt and the soft-spoken butler. It is paradoxical, in the thirtieth stanza of "Childe Roland," that the Tower should rear itself suddenly out of that unpromising wilderness, simply because the wilderness has been made to seem so unpromising. Chesterton's enthusiasm for so emotionally chaotic a poem is explicable in terms of the intuition, vivid for him and ascribed by him to Browning, that there is something paradoxical in being itself: that in the ultimate sense it is paradoxical that the Tower should rear itself suddenly anywhere. To one of proper humility, he was frequently to point out (and we shall return to this point, for it is central), it is paradoxical that there should even be such a thing as a Tower, or a stone.[15] All things burst ceaselessly upon the humble with a thrill of surprise, since they are unexpected because undeserved.

All genuine appreciation rests on a certain mystery of humility and almost of darkness. . . . The man who expects nothing sees redder roses than common men can see. . , . Blessed is he that expecteth nothing, for he shall possess the cities and the mountains; blessed is the meek, for he shall inherit the earth.[16]

Finally, this ubiquity of the paradoxical is confirmed by the very nature of speculative thought. Such thinking is basically a resolution of paradoxes, so far as it is possible to resolve them.

Truth, if it means anything at all, means the conformity of the mind with some object[17]; and thought may be described as the process by which a system of ideas is so ordered as to conform with the real system of hierarchy of things. Thinking is ordering: a resolution of the verbal and logical paradoxes that spring from disorder, frequently a convenient disorder.

We resolve a paradox in just this way whenever we make a belated identification: as when we realize that the winged mouse in our attic is a bat, or decide, from a treetop, that the great cow snorting below is a bull. Wings on the mouse, discontent in the cow, are paradoxes to be resolved: our preliminary concepts must be enlarged to accommodate them. By thus constantly enlarging our concepts to give contradictions elbow-room, we conform the order of our minds with that of things, and incidentally dull our perception of the paradoxical. The paradoxy which flourished in the patristic tradition nearly died in the scholastic: it does not altogether die in St. Thomas only because his rationalism is not sterile but rooted in a metaphysical intuition. To solve a problem is to resolve the paradox created by a previous imperfect solution. In this sense the problem is not metaphysical but of our own making, and the activity of solving it is only valuable when geared to a real metaphysical perception.

St. Thomas Aquinas was perfectly aware of this principle as he pursued through the *Summa* his invariable method of making the Fathers of the Church appear to contradict themselves, and then resolving the contradiction by properly defining the terms and arranging the ideas. St. Thomas is vital precisely because he is not spending his life harmonizing the Fathers, but rather using their statements as a point of departure for harmonizing thoughts with things. The welter of hair-line definitions and distinctions into which he is drawn prove not so much an over-subtlety about St. Thomas as an extreme unsubtlety about everyday language: unsubtle because the world is a baffling place, incapable of being enmeshed in a phrase or a formula. The greater and greater complexity of his thought is simply a series of approximations to the infinite complexity of things. Chesterton, too, saw the world in this multiple and bewildering way, as a globe that no single line of logic could encompass: for you have not seen the world when you have walked around the equator.

It is in fact through some such intuition of the contrast between sterile reason and fertile perception that the whole direction of modern philosophy has been away from reason. Bergson in particular complained that reason made reality static, and in so complaining made vivid to Jacques Maritain the folly of nineteenth-century materialistic rationalism. But Bergson went beyond reason by leaving reason behind, and it was in perceiving that metaphysical progress consisted in penetrating rather than substituting that Maritain finally broke with his master.

Maritain, in short, discovered paradox. The rationalist has not discovered it yet, and the philosophical idealist has not discovered it yet. A further useful distinction is symbolized in Maritain's abiding interest in speculative aesthetics, contrasted with Chesterton's more persistent interest in moral problems. Penetrative intuitions compatible with but not enchained by reason are the basic material of the arts, which on that level perceive and employ paradox. Chesterton, perceiving all this, penetrates beneath even this degree of formularization to a direct awareness of moral conflicts and moral implications.

It should be plain from the mere mention of Chesterton's discipleship to St. Thomas that there is no necessary antithesis between paradox and reason. The stuff of reality, which reason has somehow to discover, is paradoxical stuff. Reason is capable of telling you one thing at a time: like a line passing through Jones at one point. It would take an enormous number of points so fixed to delimit Jones, and the delimitation would be at best mechanical. Paradox consists in showing briefly and dramatically that a new line of reason will indicate a new point on the object: like being reminded, after a lifetime of concentration on Jones' face, that he has feet. It is possible, of course, simply to love without attempting to describe, and the condition of the contemplative is that of ultimately knowing (without "reconciling") all these contradictions and swallowing them up in a general love of Jones. But if the contemplative wants to communicate his vision he will have to utilize reason and speak in paradoxes.

Paradoxical stuff, then, is for Chesterton the raw material of thought; and the paradoxes arise either out of our own confusion, which thinking can more and more nearly resolve, or from the nature of Being which is unresolvable. When you have dissipated all the mists of the mind, there remains the fundamental paradox that cannot be resolved and can only be contemplated. Contemplation in this sense Chesterton called "love," and the key to his claim to be called a contemplative is contained in the statement that "we admire things with reasons, but love them without reasons,"[18] coupled with the dictum still more profound that "Man cannot love mortal things. He can only love immortal things for an instant."[19]

III: THE IDEA OF ANALOGY

HAVING FIRMLY grasped the idea that there is nothing abnormal about paradox, that indeed we use it perpetually without notice and rely on it for our literary and contemplative pleasures, we are prepared to examine more scientifically its place in language, in thought, and in reality. To do this we shall have to talk about *analogy*, the philosopher's name for the principle of which paradox is the child.[1]

Analogy runs like a thread through the whole work of St. Thomas, as paradox interpenetrates every word of Chesterton's; and just as Chesterton makes very few explicit statements about the principles of paradox, so St. Thomas, despite innumerable applications and deductions, sets forth the doctrine of analogy explicitly in only a few texts. The great commentators and elaborators of St. Thomas, however, notably Cajetan, Sylvester of Ferrara, and John of St. Thomas, supply to some extent their master's failure to treat the subject formally; while Chesterton's commentators have ignored analogy altogether, to the detriment of their understanding and treatment of his paradox.

To put the connection shortly, analogy has to do with comparison, as paradox has to do with contradiction; for putting things side by side is a necessary preliminary to having them clash.

The first point to grasp is that they do not altogether clash, or they would not both be things. The reader of Chesterton

must realize the first and simplest of the paradoxes that sit by the springs of truth. He must surely see that the fact of two things being different implies that they are similar. The hare and the tortoise may differ in the quality of swiftness, but they must agree in the quality of motion. The swiftest hare cannot be swifter than an isosceles triangle or the idea of pinkness. When we say the hare moves faster, we say that the tortoise moves. And when we say of a thing that it moves, we say, without need of other words, that there are things that do not move. And even in the act of saying that things change, we say that there is something unchangeable.[2]

Apart from the characteristic swiftness with which it arrives at the idea of God, that passage deserves attention on two counts: first, because it summarizes swiftly and brilliantly the whole idea of analogy, of likeness at the core of difference, without an understanding of which it is impossible to acquire a knowledge of metaphysics; second, because its appearance in *Heretics* in 1905 shows that Chesterton at the very beginning of his career had grasped that foundational principle and thus become, in the exact sense of the word "potential," a potential Thomist.

Analogy at its widest is concerned with the way the universe holds together: with the way things can be different and yet be things: with the way the Many participate in the One. Plainly it is a principle explicitly concerned with contradictions. The words "analogical" and "paradoxical" are, if not quite interchangeable, intimately related. Analogy explains, paradox describes; they explain and describe the same reality. It is, however, important to realize that both are tools for dealing with a metaphysical reality that can itself only be intuited. Unless sustained by vision, unless indeed employed strictly in the service of vision, the one as a means of exploring the vision, the other as a means of expressing it, they are worse than useless. A knowledge of the principle of analogy will not of itself confer an understanding of metaphysics, but only of the machinery of metaphysical analysis.

As for the principle itself, it is subtle and easily capable of misinterpretation: the most obvious error being that of Chesterton's severest critics, who ascribe to the thinker's mind the complications of clear thought. It is true that the normal mind (an exception must be made for the mystics) cannot contemplate being directly. But the fault of such heretical mystics as Blake is to be impatient with fallen man's necessarily imperfect and circumlocutory attempts to arrive at certainty by reason, and consign reason in a burst of wrath to the devil.[3] Blake abhorred long-winded thought because he had no idea how complex to other men was the reality with which he was so familiarly and immediately confronted. The critic of Chesterton, at the other end of the scale, is impatient with paradoxes because he has no idea of the complexity of a reality he has never intuited. The beginner in metaphysics, finally, is susceptible to a third and subtler but exactly parallel error; struck by the simplicity of the analogical proportion-sum, he imagines that if his mind were only a little more capacious he could form a clear and distinct idea of being. The trouble, he thinks, and the heretical mystic thinks, and the unsuspecting critic thinks, lies in the mind.

The trouble, however, lies in reality itself; and is summarized in the statement that *being is intrinsically analogical.*[4]

The tendency toward these errors may be discerned in a simple example. Man is said to be good; similarly, God is said to be good. It is plainly folly, however, to say that man is therefore as good as God.

The obvious, and the wrong, resolution of this paradox is to say that it springs from a difficulty of vocabulary. If we had only enough words to express gradations of goodness, it may be thought, we could

escape the paradox by predicating one word of God
and another of man. God, we might say, is good; and
man is glugg. Or we might place the difficulty solely
in the limitations of the human intelligence; we have
derived a conception of goodness from our experience
with man, and must expand it beyond all intellectual
grasp to include God. One man's hand can only
manage five-finger exercises at either end of a gigantic keyboard; he can call a man good, and he can call
God good. He cannot span them.

Attractive as these dodges are, they are plainly
circular. They involve abandoning any notion of
likeness between man and God, or else insisting
only on the likeness and trying to cover up the
difference with different words. They attempt to
dodge the real problem of diversity in likeness, which
is rooted in two beings, man and God.

The answer of St. Thomas and of Chesterton is
that goodness is possessed by man and by God, but
not in the same way. The way in which men are
good is proportionate to the being which men have;
the way in which God is good is proportionate to
the being which God has.

The reader who objects to metaphysical consid-
erations involving God may like to be reminded that
the classical ideal of decorum betrays a parallel
intuition. When we urge a child to be decorous we
do not expect him to behave in the same way as an

equally decorous Prime Minister: we expect him to behave as a child should behave, and imply that the Prime Minister behaves as a Prime Minister should behave. There is difference, and there is also a certain likeness. The word "decorum" is analogical. It means behaviour proper to one's being. Where Chesterton transcended the average classical scholar was in his perception of decorum on a moral and metaphysical plane.

Angels know as angels are; men know as men are. Confronted with the angelic knowledge, one is guilty of paradox in saying that men know at all. But the paradox is not the fault of the speaker, or of his vocabulary. It is rooted in the being of men and of angels. In this way knowledge is analogical, and goodness, and beauty, and every other perfection of being.[5] At this level one may resolve the greater part of Chesterton's explicit paradoxes. Take decorum again: "Decorum is not tame," he writes; "decorum is wild, as wild as the wind in the night."[6] But it is plain that the wildness of decorum is the wildness with which a man binds himself by one pattern of behaviour when he might be sampling twenty million. It is the wildness of a rash vow. The pattern of decorum is tame in the sense that he never leaves it; it is wild in the sense that he always might. The word is analogical, and therein lies its shifting mystery.

To begin to plumb Chesterton's metaphysical depths, however, it is necessary to carry the principle of analogy one stage farther. Too much cannot be made of the continual rapture with which the contemplation of things inspires him: trees and lampposts and hackney cabs and horses and all the other works of God.[7] And the reason that they are wonderful is that they *are*: they participate in being.

Everything that is is wrapped in the mystery of its own incommunicable individuality, and hence all things are wonderfully different; but everything that is exercises the act of existence in common with everything else, and in that sense all things are alike. Both the wonder of differentiation and the wonderful fact of existence are explained and illuminated by the Thomistic ascription of difference to the individual essences of things, in proportion to which they exercise the act of existence. The grass exists grassily, the cloud cloudily; they both are, and they are both different, according to the way in which they are.

Chesterton illuminates this fundamental concept of Thomistic metaphysics in his *St. Thomas Aquinas*, in a passage of unique importance: it unites in Chesterton's perception St. Thomas, the idea of analogy, the intuition of being, and that wide-eyed wonder at the multiplicity of the universe which is the distinguishing mark of Chesterton's life and writing:

Aquinas has affirmed that our first sense of fact is a fact; and he cannot go back on it without falsehood. But when we come to look at the fact or facts, as we know them, we observe that they have a rather queer character; which has made many moderns grow strangely restless and sceptical about them. For instance, they are largely in a state of change, from being one thing to being another; or their qualities are relative to other things; or they appear to move incessantly; or they appear to vanish entirely. At this point, as I say, many sages lose hold of the first principle of reality, which they would concede at first; and fall back on saying that there is nothing except change; or nothing except comparison; or nothing except flux; or in effect that there is nothing at all. Aquinas turns the whole argument the other way, keeping in line with his first realization of reality. There is no doubt about the being of being, even if it does sometimes look like becoming; that is because what we see is not the fullness of being; or (to continue a sort of colloquial slang) we never see being being as much as it can. Ice is melted into cold water, and cold water is heated into hot water; it cannot be all three at once. But this does not make water unreal or even relative; it only means that its being is limited to being one thing at a time. But the fullness of being is everything that can be; and without it the lesser and approximate forms of being cannot be explained as anything; unless they are explained away as nothing. . . .

St. Thomas maintains that the ordinary thing at every moment is something; but it is not everything that it could be. There is a fullness of being, in which it could be everything that it can be. Thus, while most sages come at last to nothing but naked change, he comes to the ultimate thing that is unchangeable, because it is all the other things at once. While they describe a change which is really a change in nothing, he describes a changelessness which includes the changes of everything. Things change because they are not complete; but their reality can only be explained as part of something that is complete. It is God. . . .

The defect we see, in what is, is simply that it is not all that is. God is more actual even than Man; more actual even than Matter; for God with all His powers at every instant is immortally in action.[8]

It is in this way that Chesterton sees paradox rooted in being, and the created world rooted in God; so that he could never see a lamp-post without the instinct to praise.[9] "I believe," he wrote, "about the universal cosmos, or for that matter about every weed and pebble in the cosmos, that men will never rightly realize that it is beautiful, until they realize that it is strange. . . . Poetry is the separation of the soul from some object, whereby we can regard it with wonder."[10] With the sense of strangeness came the sense of gratitude; not only because, amid so many potentialities, the object at hand might not have been, but also because in its limited being it participated in all Being: in God. He was thankful for a lamp-post because it was not a limpet, but he would have been equally thankful for a limpet.

Before he had discovered the idea of analogy,

he had discovered the need of thankfulness; between the ages of twenty and twenty-four he wrote in his Notebook,

You say grace before meals
    All right.
But I say grace before the play and the opera,
And grace before the concert and pantomime,
And grace before I open a book,
And grace before sketching, painting,
Swimming, fencing, walking, boxing, playing, dancing,
And grace before I dip the pen in the ink.[11]

And again,

I thank thee, O Lord, for the stones in the street
I thank thee for the hay-carts yonder and for the houses
    built and half-built
That fly past me as I stride.
But most of all for the great wind in my nostrils
As if thine own nostrils were close.[12]

And at the end of his life, in the final chapter of the *Autobiography*, he sums up all that he has ever thought, coming again by a series of stupendous leaps from the idea of gratitude to the idea of God:

I began in my boyhood to grope for (the truth) from quite the other end; the end of the earth most remote from purely supernatural hopes. But even about the dimmest earthly hope or the smallest earthly happiness, I had from the first an almost violently vivid sense of these two dangers; the sense that the experience must not be spoiled by presumption or despair. To take a convenient tag out of my first juvenile book of rhymes,

I asked through what incarnations or pre-natal purga-
tories I must have passed to gain the reward of looking
at a dandelion. . . . What I said about the dandelion
is exactly what I should say about the sunflower or the
sun, or the glory which (as the poet said) is brighter
than the sun. The only way to enjoy even a weed is to
feel unworthy even of a weed. . . .

Uncreated man, merely in the position of the babe
unborn, has no right even to see a dandelion; for he
could not himself have invented either the dandelion
or the eyesight. . . .

This common human mysticism about the dust or the
dandelion or the daily life of man does depend and
always did depend on theology, if it dealt at all in
thought. And if it be next asked why this theology,
I answer here—because it is the only theology that has
not only thought, but thought of everything.[13]

And clinching the argument he states as strongly
and briefly as he ever did state it the old Thomistic
principle of analogy, which he had hurled against
the sceptics of 1905:

The agreement we really want is the agreement between agreement and disagreement. It is the sense that
things do really differ, though they are at one.[14]

Continually in this way he reverts to being: being
wherein the things that differ are at one; continually
in this way does he thank All Being for the multiplicity of beings. This is an important contemplative
idea; its importance however for the present argument is the proof it furnishes that Chesterton's
metaphysical intuition *was* intuitive and inclusive.

The man who wrote, "God is more actual even than Man; more actual even than Matter; for God with all His powers at every instant is immortally in action," put clearly a point that the merely deductive metaphysician cannot put at all. One may thus put the analogical principle in its simplest form by saying that Chesterton, like the Fathers and the mediaeval allegorizers, perceived the world as a "divine animal," a network of analogies; had, it may be said, an instinct for Being: without which instinct men are not philosophers, conscious of what is, but mere logicians, conscious of relations between appearances. It was ultimately this instinct for being, this perception of the organic and the corresponding horror of the analytic, that divided the angry Blake from the world:

. . . Reasonings like vast serpents
Infold around my limbs, bruising my minute articulations.

I turn my eyes to the schools & Universities of Europe
And there behold the loom of Locke, whose woof
    rages dire
Wash'd by the Water-wheels of Newton; black the cloth
In heavy wreathes folds over every Nation: cruel Works
Of many Wheels I view, wheel without wheel, with
    cogs tyrannic
Moving by compulsion each other, not as those in Eden
    which
Wheel within Wheel, in freedom revolve in harmony
    & peace.[15]

It is this instinct for Being which sounds through poetry the note of wonder and of intricate allegory. Chesterton says,

> Until we realize that things might not be, we cannot realize that things are. Until we see the background of darkness, we cannot admire the light as a single and created thing. As soon as we have seen that darkness, all light is lightning, sudden, blinding, and divine. Until we picture nonentity, we underrate the victory of God, and can realize none of the trophies of His ancient war. It is one of the million wild jests of truth, that we know nothing until we know nothing.[16]

The tradition in which he is working here equally sustains Traherne:

> I that so long
>   Was nothing from eternity
> Did little think such joys of ear and tongue
>   To celebrate or see:
> Such sounds to hear, such hands to feel, such feet,
> Beneath the skies on such a ground to meet. . . .
>
>   From dust I rise
>   And out of nothing now awake,
> These brighter regions which salute mine eyes,
>   A gift from God I take.
> The earth, the seas, the light, the day, the skies,
> The sun and stars are mine; if those I prize.[17]

This wonder begotten of the contrast between something and nothing is complemented in such passages as this of Crashaw, which with the same instinct for being exploit a ramification of organic analogies in the "something," and frequently justify literally the literary historian's adjective Metaphysical:

> Hail, sister springs,
> Parents of silver-footed rills!
> Ever-bubbling things,
> Thawing crystal, snowy hills!
> Still spending, never spent; I mean
> Thy fair eyes, sweet Magdelene.
>
> Heavens thy fair eyes be;
> Heavens of ever-falling stars;
> 'Tis seed-time still with thee,
> And stars thou sowest whose harvest dares
> Promise the earth to countershine
> Whatever makes Heaven's forehead fine. . . .[18]

In the same spirit and from the same perception Tertullian in his treatise on the Resurrection of the Flesh invokes the allegory of natural resurrection not to illustrate but actually to prove the theological doctrine:

Day dies into night, and is buried everywhere in darkness . . . But yet it again revives, with its own beauty its own dowry, its own sun, the same as ever . . . slaying its own death, night—opening its own sepulchre, the darkness—coming forth the heir to itself. . . . Nothing perishes but with a view to salvation. The whole, therefore, of this revolving order of things bears witness to the resurrection of the dead.[19]

It is the same instinct for being, less rationalized and more akin to simple wonder, that led the Elizabethan poets into catalogues, inviting their readers to share the simple pleasure of naming over created things:

Much can they praise the trees so straight and hy,
The sayling Pine; the Cedar proud and tall;
The vine-prop Elme; the Poplar never dry;
The builder Oake, sole king of forrests all;
The Aspine good for staves; the Cypresse funerall;[20]

and so on for nine more lines. It was the instinct for
being, manifesting itself in a similar pattern, that
led James Joyce, reviving in our own day the patristic
tradition, to pack into his vast celebration of the One
a multitude of names of particulars; that led him to
weave into the river-chapter of *Finnegans Wake* the
names of five hundred rivers; that led him to cram
the long self-vindication of the Prince of the Natural
World, Haveth Childers Everywhere, with so many
names of particular natural objects as to render the
voice of Nature, always blurred, nearly unintelli-
gible; and that elevates to poetic rhetoric the earthy
Molly Bloom at the end of *Ulysses*:

I love flowers Id love to have the whole place swimming in roses God of heaven theres nothing like nature
the wild mountains then the sea and the waves rushing
then the beautiful country with fields of oats and wheat
and all kinds of things and all the fine cattle going
about that would do your heart good to see rivers and
lakes and flowers all sorts of shapes and smells and
colours springing up even out of the ditches primroses
and violets. . . .[21]

It is the instinct for being, finally, which leads to
a love even of ugly things, and led Browning to that
celebration of the "ragged thistle-stalk" and "the

dock's harsh swarth leaves, bruised as to balk all
hope of greenness"[22] whereon Chesterton ringingly
commented:

> "What does the poem of 'Childe Roland' mean?"
> The only genuine answer to this is, "What does any-
> thing mean? Does the earth mean nothing? Do grey
> skies and wastes covered with thistles mean nothing?
> Does an old horse turned out to graze mean nothing?
> If it does, there is but one further truth to be added—
> that everything means nothing.[23]

It is indeed the ultimate corollary of the instinct
for being that everything is meaningful because
being is organic and ultimately one. While Chesterton in simple wonder "will never let us forget that if
man made gargoyles, God made the hippopotamus,"[24]
and remarks of a kindred brute, "It is one thing to
describe an interview with a gorgon or a griffin, a
creature who does not exist; it is another thing to
discover that the rhinoceros does exist and then take
pleasure in the fact that he looks as if he didn't;"[25]
yet his more valuable perceptions transcend simple
wonder to comprehend by analogies the monstrous
paradoxes of Scripture about saving life by losing it
and inheriting the earth by being unworthy of it,
and with Blake

> To see a World in a Grain of Sand
> And Heaven in a Wild Flower,
> Hold Infinity in the palm of your hand
> And Eternity in an hour.[26]

IV: THE WORD

IT WOULD have been both inviting and dangerous to commence the examination of Chesterton's paradoxes with his puns; inviting because the pun is the foundation of his humour and through his analogical perceptions inextricably mixed with his thought; dangerous because word-play of all the forms of paradox balances most precariously on the knife-edge between the perfunctory and the profound. It was Chesterton's misfortune in his youth to be contemporary with the last decadents, who had grown tired of calling grass green and were busily exploiting the keen but, as it proved, quickly exhaustible pleasure of calling it grey.[1] It was his misfortune because he could only express the heights of rapture by the same device the decadents used to express the depths of boredom; and the reading public was a long time finding out the difference. It is fatally easy for the writer to make a paradox, and dreadfully difficult for the reader to tell whether it is a sound one; especially when the reader has been brought up, like the Edwardians, on Scientific

Method and clear and distinct ideas, and is accustomed to suspecting poetry and paradox on principle. Thus Oscar Wilde's character could remark with a yawn, "Those who are faithful know only the trivial side of love; it is the faithless who know love's tragedies,"[2] and Chesterton on the contrary could exclaim, "Decorum is not tame, decorum is wild, as wild as the wind in the night. . . . Modesty is too fierce and elemental a thing for the modern pedants to understand. . . . It has in it the joy of escape and the ancient shyness of freedom";[3] and on the surface who is to judge between them? Both appear to be standing some truth on its head to attract attention.

That is exactly what they are doing. They are using paradox here, Chesterton also, as a means of rhetorical persuasion. Here in the Chesterton passage the moral intuition has retreated into the background; the statement is true, but the purpose in its phrasing is not primarily truthfulness but effect.

It is extraordinarily difficult to disentangle this merely rhetorical use of paradox from the metaphysical perception that underlies everything Chesterton said; and there is a parallel difficulty in discovering how far his puns are merely play and how far they are involved in the ancient verbalist tradition of scriptural exegesis. The attempt must nevertheless be made, if only to highlight the pervasive metaphysical basis of his work; and it is not an impossible attempt. The distinctions are valid, though the evidence is thoroughly confused. Rhetorical paradox and the passing joke may strictly be said to depend upon the word and not the world; the confusion is due to the fact that a thorough analogical perception of the world also includes the word. Like Vico, Chesterton treats language as a bridge between the human microcosm and the world; language has a consistency of its own—ultimately, an autonomy—derived from its function of mediating between the mind and the universe. The body of language is an organic body because the mind is an organic body and the universe is an organic body.

Assuming a sound moral conscience, the only possible justification for paradox is that what it says is true. But what language says is not always what it seems to say: an Indian is not a Red Man, and a Locomotive is not an Iron Horse. Such verbal paradox is thus less description than a sort of gesture, intended to recommend certain aspects of the Indian and the Locomotive to the attention of the reader.

We have already said that verbal paradox can be escaped, while metaphysical cannot; and it is important to understand why. The words of a proper metaphysical paradox express concepts framed from the perception of being, which is intrinsically analogical. Peter is tall compared to other men and tiny compared to the elephant; to see his neighbours he looks both up and down; he is both tall and short at the same time; and there is the end of it. If you are including in your synthesis mankind, Peter, and the elephant you cannot avoid using expressions of size analogically; that is, paradoxically. But if you leave the elephant out of it and restrict your consideration to mankind, you can call Peter tall without ambiguity. He is a tall man. He is tall as men go. He is tall in proportion to his being: his human being. Now verbal paradox consists in leaving the elephant out of it, and yet maintaining, for special rhetorical purposes, that Peter is short.

The special rhetorical purpose of Chesterton is to overcome the mental inertia of human beings, which mental inertia is constantly landing them in the strange predicament of both seeing a thing and not seeing it. When people's perceptions are in this condition, they must, in the strictest sense of the words, be made to renew their acquaintance with things. They must be made to see them anew, as if for the first time.[4] Now a man's acquaintance with truth is likely to be renewed by the violent shock of being told a thundering and obvious lie. If we call Peter short, people may really realize that he is tall.

The possible reasons for calling Peter short are therefore twofold: paradox for the sake of recalling a forgotten truth, and paradox for the sake of placing the discussion of Peter in a metaphysical context.

The former can be managed without a show of paradox if the words be adroitly chosen, and paradox
when employed in this first way is employed at the
discretion of the writer as a rhetorical device. The
latter cannot but be paradoxical; as long as the
elephant and Peter's brother are both included in
the synthesis, Peter will be both tall and short at the
same time, in two different contexts that are really
one context. Paradox employed in this second way
is based on a metaphysical intuition that sees more
than other men see; it is only surprising to the reader
who cannot see the elephant.

Chesterton is generally paradoxical because he
sees more than other men see. His whole habit of
thought, whose history, as we have shown, began
with thankfulness, impelled him to see not lamp-
posts but limited beings participating in All Being;
he was accustomed to looking at grass and seeing
God. And the consciousness of God introduces another dimension into the consideration of grass, just
as the inclusion of the elephant introduces another
dimension into the measurement of Peter. Chesterton was continually talking in paradoxes because
he was perceiving analogically, seeing each separate
thing in its metaphysical context.

There should by now be no difficulty in disen-
tangling from the Chestertonian corpus this principle
of analogical perception, whose key is not the word

but the world, and reserving it for future treatment. Our business here is with verbal paradox, whose use is rhetorical.

Verbal paradox consists in telling people that they are wrong, casting the contradiction into a limited and therefore artistic form; or else in startling them into realizing what you are actually saying. It bespeaks Chesterton's sincerity that he very seldom speaks merely to startle, or to make people listen to what he is going to say next. When he does, it is because he seeks hearers for a worthy argument, or because he cannot resist a passing joke. "The preaching friar," he remarks, "puts his sermon into popular language, the missionary fills his sermon with anecdotes and even jokes, because he is thinking of his mission and not of himself. . . . The Apostles' Creed begins with the pronoun 'I'; but it goes on to rather more important names and nouns."[5]

The passing joke we shall consider shortly; our first business is with the paradox offered in flat contradiction of current opinion. Of this sort are his exposures of popular euphemisms (Companionate Marriage, "so-called because the people involved are not married and will very rapidly cease to be companions") and popular proverbs ("If a thing is worth doing it is worth doing badly").[6] Of this sort also is the following climax of a train of argument in defense of general ideas:

The opportunist politician is like one who should abandon billiards because he was beaten at billiards, and abandon golf because he was beaten at golf. There is nothing which is so weak for working purposes as this enormous importance attached to immediate victory. *There is nothing that fails like success.*[7]

Such a reversal of a popular saying he commonly holds in reserve in just this way, and springs as an epigrammatic summary at the climax of a general argument. A typical paragraph in *Heretics* sets out to refute Kipling's celebrated query, "What can they know of England who only England know?" Chesterton commences by pointing out that the world does not include England any more than it includes the Church, and developing his favorite theme of the separateness of things he demonstrates that knowledge comes not from surveying but from penetration of particulars in an analogical framework. The argument so far is metaphysical, but the concluding epigram is rhetorical and effectively astonishing: "The globe-trotter lives in a smaller world than the peasant."[8]

However rhetorical may be the particular devices, particular epigrams, the argument is always metaphysical; which is what justifies the devices. The reader may like to try his wits on the following:

But if you are to have anything like divine discontent, then it must really be divine. Anything that comes from below must really come from above.[9]

* * *

(Blake) had not the independence, one might almost say the omnipotence, that comes from being hopelessly weak.[10]

* * *

(The Tolstoyans) will not be improved by plain living and high thinking. They . . . would be improved by high living and plain thinking.[11]

* * *

The New Paganism is no longer new, and never at any time bore the smallest resemblance to Paganism. . . . The term "pagan" is continually used in fiction and light literature as meaning a man without any religion, whereas a pagan was generally a man with about half a dozen.[12]

* * *

Critics say that his visions were false because he was mad. I say he was mad because his visions were true.[13]

* * *

Blasphemy is not wild; blasphemy is in its nature prosaic. It consists in regarding in a commonplace manner something which other and happier people regard in a rapturous and imaginative manner.[14]

* * *

What ruins mankind is the ignorance of the expert.[15]

* * *

To make the rhetorical function of verbal paradox clear beyond dispute, we shall examine in some detail the working of one of these examples. It is first necessary to point out that the distinction made above between two kinds of verbal paradox, that which is flung in flat contradiction of the reader, and that which contradicts fact for the purpose of arousing readers to a realization of their own perception of the fact, is speculative rather than real. Both are rhetorical functions, and both in practice are generally joined in a single specimen of verbal paradox.

To see how Chesterton is contradicting fact at the same time that he is ostensibly contradicting his readers, we must recall that a paradox has by definition two contrasting halves. One half is here the statement of Chesterton; the other is the contrary belief of the reader, which is founded on fact, though not adequate to the fact. Chesterton is always coherent and lucid, but the reader's fixed and contrary ideas are not infrequently just as coherent and lucid. Chesterton's contradictions are democratic because respectful; he grants that the reader is as right as himself. Take the example of blasphemy:

> Blasphemy is not wild; blasphemy is in its nature prosaic. It consists in regarding in a commonplace manner something which other and happier people regard in a rapturous and imaginative manner.

Now it is perfectly plain that blasphemy *is* wild, because it shocks. Chesterton's primary purpose is equally plain. He is thwacking vigorously at a public that was appeasing its thirst for shock by applauding blasphemy. Blasphemy, he would grant, is exciting;

but orthodoxy, he would insist, is more exciting. The word "blasphemy" and the word "excitement" have become so intermixed in the public mind that he can only sunder them by insisting violently on that side of blasphemy that is not exciting at all. That is, as we have said, his primary purpose; but he has another and less obvious purpose, which is to remind his readers that blasphemy after all *is* exciting, even if it is a forbidden excitement. Startled by the slap of this unfamiliar contradiction, the reader recalls with horror that blasphemy is something more than a diversion for bored aesthetes. His avowed attitude to blasphemy is that it is shocking, and Chesterton would startle him out of that, lest he seek those shocks. But his real and practical attitude to blasphemy is probably that he does not care tuppence whether Oscar Wilde blasphemes or not; and Chesterton wants to startle him out of that too. ("I believe in preaching to the converted," he remarks, "for I have generally found that the converted do not understand their own religion.")[16] Chesterton's explicit contradiction accomplishes one end; his readers' startled, half-conscious reaffirmation of what is contradicted accomplishes the other. The paradox not only sets right thinking that was wrong, but recalls to a sense of its own rightness that part of public thinking that is unconsciously right.

The difficulty many experience in reading Chesterton, especially in reading the earlier works which contain a far higher proportion of verbal paradoxes than do the later and calmer ones, does not arise out of any vagueness in Chesterton's meaning, for there is never any difficulty in seeing what he means. The difficulty arises from the exhaustion of combat: from trying to bear one's beliefs erect through the storms of a relentless topsy-turvydom.

One may deduce from this experience that the kind of folly Chesterton is opposing in such paradoxes is the folly of thinking in words, of mistaking words for things; of clinging to a slogan, to what Mr. A. P. Herbert excellently calls a "witch-word," because it appears to be the result of ordered thinking. So long as you are aware that what you say is a consequence of what you see and think, says Chesterton, you are in no peril. Your peril commences when you abandon the world and clutch blindly at the word.

The word is good, but the word can devour the mind. Chesterton's homage to words is incessant and even immoderate: the quest of the passing pun is strictly speaking a major blemish on his literary style. It never, however, blemishes his thinking; a contemplative before he was an artist, he keeps his puns very firmly where they belong, on the level of artistic execution.

This proposition is strongly unacceptable to the modern mind, disabused as it is of any respect for puns by the whole tradition of English prose since the Restoration. So miraculously do Chesterton's puns, alliterations, rhymes, and echoes support and reinforce his matter that grave scholarly doubts about a man thinking merely in verbalisms have pursued him since his career began. Assessing the drag of this false accusation upon Chesterton's chances for literary survival, Belloc reflects,

It would have been better, perhaps, had he never fallen into verbalism (wherein he tended to exceed). For fools were led thereby to think that he was merely verbalist whereas he was in reality a thinker so profound and so direct that he had no equal.

Anyhow, verbalist he was. It was his superficial defect. . . . Chesterton, being verbalist, was in most of his books (of Essays at least) perpetually punning. Now the teachers of the human race often exceeded in the direction of punning. The fathers of the Church were always at it (among whom I may quote the old tag: "Non est mendacium sed mysterium"—which is, I believe, St. Augustine. Let me also quote "Mutans Evae Nomen." I spare you five hundred others.)

To revel in words is the mark of a master of words. The great Rabelais will nod and approve this verdict from his throne in heaven. It is no wonder that Chesterton with his magnificent exuberance should exceed where words are concerned and thereby fall into punning, which trope is based on the word suggesting the word. But I always wish, when I am reading him, that he had avoided the temptation, and had concentrated upon direct exposition, wherein, like his contemporary H. G. Wells, he was a master.[17]

Belloc nowhere shows to better advantage his sound historical sense than in thus placing Chesterton in the tradition of punning represented by the Fathers of the Church. There is a translatable example in Tertullian, who comments on Aaron's command that the earrings of the women be thrown into the fire, that "the people were about to lose, as a judgment upon themselves, the true ornaments for the ears, the words of God."[18] The tradition is to be found continued in English in such sermons as those of Lancelot Andrewes, who comments on the lottery between Haman and Mordecai,

There is no cause, no means in a lot. It is St. Augustine's note, that it is therefore termed "the lot of the righteous," in the Psalm, and in the Apostle *sors sanctorum*, for that merit or means there is none at all: God only allots it to us. And such was ours: not by means, as they; but delivered, as I may say, from a lot, by a lot, a mere lot. So our Purim, we may say, was more pure than theirs.[19]

And the reader will not forget the pun on which, as Chesterton somewhere remarks, the Church was founded: *Tu es Petrus.*

It is in fact almost impossible to find in Chesterton naked examples of the passing joke. His jokes are so intermixed with his habit of exposition by parallel—a parallel not by him made, but perceived—

with his perception of the "joky" aspect of creation,
and with his habit of worshipping created things,
including things whereof he is himself the inter-
mediate creator, by lingering on them and allowing
them to move him to laughter, that one can scarcely
say of any given remark that it was only put there
for fun. The traditional network of analogies which
Chesterton intuited in being embraces not only
metaphysics but grammar and philology: and he is
squarely in the Christian patristic tradition of philo-
logical exegesis.

To point to a revival of this patristic tradition
is one way of explaining certain modern literary
trends. Chesterton displays, in common with the
whole modern resurrection of art, an almost mystical
veneration for his materials. Words are magical:
words *are*. The word "tree" is not merely a counter
or a pointer: it exists as an object, in all the analogical splendour of being, just as the tree itself exists.[20]
A cardinal principle of the entire modern literary
movement, from Hopkins and Eliot to Stein and
Joyce, is to exploit the individual existences of individual words. Mr. Eliot ordering his oaken varia-
tions:

> Because I do not hope to turn again
> Because I do not hope
> Because I do not hope to turn . . . ;

Miss Stein delightedly caressing words with her pen:

Saint Therese. Who settles a private life.
Saint Therese.
Saint Therese. Who settles a private life.
        Enact end of an act;

young Joyce conning a phrase drawn from his treasury:

A day of dappled seaborne clouds;[21]

the mature Joyce devoting the final third of his life to a towering edifice of multilingual puns: all of them are working in a tradition forgotten since Miltonic thunders obliterated the sensibility that could relish "Brightness falls from the air."

Joyce, who of all the moderns would seem to totter most sickeningly on the brink of contriving mere crossword puzzles, blinded himself to that danger by his strong act of faith in a mysterious relationship, persistent in a long tradition through the Fathers from Plato's *Cratylus,* between the word and the essence of the thing. Chesterton's delighted punning, like Shakespeare's, seems to share some sense of that dim mirroring. The Church, he remarks, was founded on a pun; and there is a bed-rock rightness about being able to round off a comparison between the moon and cold hard reason with an allusion to the moon as the mother of lunatics[22] that suggests, and certainly suggested to him, some immense, indiscoverable harmony between words and things and actions and ideas whereof every sound work of art is but the revelation of some tiny corner. It is unnecessary to call in evidence the reference in *George Frederick Watts* to "the general hypothesis of a possible kinship between pictorial and moral harmonies in the psychology of men";[23] that he at least half accepted so vast a network of correspondences is plain from the way he fits squarely into the patristic tradition, and from the very nature of his analogical perception.

Writing in haste and without a trace of that arrogance which is the surest spur to artistic preciosity, Chesterton pains his fastidious readers with blemish after blemish: generally, be it noted, an excellent epigram drawn out too long, like the essay in *Sidelights* which hunts the idea of "keeping your hair on" through every conceivable variation (though, curiously enough, baldness vs. bushy hair was a favorite theme of the Renaissance literary virtuosos, who delighted in paradox as a means of rhetorical display).[24] But every reader open at all to logic can sympathize with his exuberance without supposing that riotous word-play is being passed off as thought. Chesterton is one of the sanest, if not most aesthetically satisfying, of modern writers, because amid all the chaos of methodological discovery he is never overwhelmed by his methods. To abandon altogether the world for the word is as fatal to art as to thinking. It is the aesthetic error of Gertrude Stein, just as the equation of "blasphemy" and "excitement" consti-

tuted a logical error on the part of Chesterton's
Edwardian public.

We have shown how these words (for example)
had become so inextricably mixed up in the public
mind that Chesterton was forced to take up the
sword of surprise to sunder them. We have also
shown that these connected words no longer represented any real attitude to blasphemy, so that he
was forced to remind the reader that blasphemy
was exciting, in the very act of telling him that it
was not. It is not difficult to see that the ill requiring
so complex a surgery arose from the reader's habit
of merely linking words, of saying "blasphemy is
wild" with no clearer idea of reality than if he had
said "bluebottles are welcome." The verbal paradox
is simply a weapon for overcoming mental laziness.

It takes two to play this kind of game, and it is
essential that both parties bear in mind the sense in
which it is a game. Chesterton and his reader are
like two men locked in each other's arms, rocking
back and forth in an effort to regain balance. The
reader must remember, as Chesterton does, that the
object of the game is balance and not rocking. "Men
who cannot taste a truth unless it be highly seasoned
with epigram and shock," observes Belloc, "will
misunderstand his manner because it will satisfy
them for the wrong reason."[25] He might have added
that it will also dissatisfy many other men, also for
the wrong reason. Since verbal paradox can always

be avoided through the right choice of language (being, in fact, simply a conscious strategy), Chesterton might have said any of these things in a way that would have startled nobody. He did not, because the kind of success he sought, the success of conviction by illumination rather than mere acquiescence or apprehension, could only be achieved by startling; and if certain readers are startled into disgust, he cannot help that. A desperate surgeon, he either cures or kills.

To sum up: verbal paradox is the artist's prerogative, because the artist with a specific aim to accomplish uses it knowingly to persuade, while anyone else may avoid it if he chooses. Its method is to exploit the double senses analogically possessed by single words; the principle, in other words, is always, in some form or other, the pun, and by way of the pun Chesterton is heir to a long tradition; for to perceive puns is ultimately to perceive a totality of words and things and feelings analogically. His use of the verbal paradox is always intricate and multiple, because to use it simply, to correct on one page and to startle on another, is to assume that the reader is sometimes wholly wrong and at other times wholly asleep. It is a mark both of his great humility and of his great psychological insight that he makes no such assumption: he was too proudly a democrat to postulate such total depravity in the image of God.

V: THE WORLD

DESPITE HIS jokes, despite his ironies, verbalisms, embroideries, and crudities, Chesterton is almost never concerned with weaving graceful patterns in the world of appearances. In the long "Apology for Buffoons" that introduces *The Well and the Shallows,* he gives a mock example of the "truly beautiful essay," which "generally deals with experiences of a certain unprovocative sort in a certain unattached fashion":

> The pond in my garden shows, under the change of morning, an apprehension of the moving air, hardly to be called a wave; and so little clouding its lucidity as to seem rather vacuity in motion. Here at least is nothing to stain the bright negation of water; none of those suburban gold-fish that look like carrots and do but nose after their tails in a circle of frustration, to give some sulky gardener cause to cry "stinking fish." The mind is altogether carried away by the faint curve of wind over water; the movement is something less solid than anything we can call liquid . . .[1]

and so on. Without at this stage begging the question of art, one may say briefly that this aesthetic concern with the pattern of appearances is in Chesterton's view dangerous because it comes to be mistaken for an end; it is dangerous to dally with words and thoughts, for lingering among these we may forfeit the vision of reality. In the same essay he says:

Nobody has yet made an adequate study of the effect of mere phonetics in confusing logic and misleading philosophers. And the worst of that sort of danger is that it is deep and subtle. To decorate an argument with puns and verbal tricks may be a superficial folly. But it is better than the sort of folly that is not superficial.[2]

We shall commence our exploration of Chesterton's metaphysical intuition with this ancient problem of getting past the appearances of things. In a sense it is true to say that Chesterton solved it, as did St. Thomas Aquinas, by the principle of analogy;[3] in another sense his immediate and penetrating vision never perceived that there was a problem. He rehearses no solution, because he needed none; he is only aware of the problem at all when he is discussing the struggles of other philosophers.

It is clear from Chesterton's discussions of the point in *Heretics* and *St. Thomas Aquinas* that he recognizes two traditional solutions to the problem of eluding the trap of appearances: a rational and an intuitive solution, that of the mind and that of the eyes. Either you reason your way beyond the Many to the One, or you see the One immediately beyond the Many. The danger of the visionary approach is illusion, and of the rational approach sterility. It is the latter danger, attending the latter approach, that most concerns Chesterton: Chesterton, who was reared in the company of the last lingering giants of Victorian rationalism and saw as a young man their winged reason beating its pinions in the void and slumping into scepticism and despair.

All his early work is scarred with impatient rebellion against the "thought that stops thought."[4] In *Orthodoxy* he cries:

> That is the ultimate evil against which all religious authority was aimed. It only appears at the end of decadent ages like our own; and already Mr. Wells has raised its ruinous banner; he has written a delicate piece of scepticism called "Doubts of the Instrument." In this he questions the brain itself, and endeavours to remove all reality from all his own assertions, past, present, and to come.[5]

In succeeding changes he catalogues rapidly the fruits of reason decayed as they hung on the sterile branches of 1908: the extreme evolutionary hypothesis that there is "only one thing, and that is a flux of anything and everything," and hence "no things to think about";[6] the ancient nominalistic denial of categories, destructive because "thinking means connecting things, and stops if they cannot be connected";[7] the theory of progress, "which maintains that we alter the test instead of trying to pass the test . . . like discussing whether Milton was more puritanical than a pig is fat";[8] pragmatism, which "tells a man to think what he must think and never mind the Absolute"—"a kind of verbal paradox" because "pragmatism is a matter of human needs, and one of the first human needs is to be something more than a pragmatist";[9] finally, the attempt to "break out of the doomed fortress of rationalism" by the doctrine of "the divine authority of will"; a sortie doomed in itself because "to admire mere choice is to refuse to choose."[10]

"The mere questioner," therefore, "has knocked his head against the limits of human thought; and cracked it."[11] He is a "mere" questioner, that is, a mere rationalist, because he lacks what we have elsewhere called the instinct for being, and what Chesterton before he knew the Thomistic vocabulary called "Mysticism."[12] Mysticism properly denotes an altogether supra-rational mode of supernatural experience, and Chesterton never was nor claimed to be a Mystic, in the sense that St. John of the Cross was a mystic, or St. Theresa. His use of the wrong word to express something of which he was acutely conscious but for which he did not yet know the right word has given critics cause to align him with the deniers of reason; just as the very similar linguistic lapse of that framer of supremely rational systems, Blake, has laid him open to a similar imputation.[13] But anyone taking the body of Chesterton's work as a whole, or even a book like *Orthodoxy* as a whole, will see that his complaint is not against Reason *per se* but against reason unfertilized by reality: against the rationalist who lacks the instinct for being.

Now because being is intrinsically analogical, reason describing being is led into paradox. And hence, because language is rational, writing in touch with reality is supremely paradoxical.

We shall come to plenty of examples in a moment. Let us first recapitulate the original problem of perceiving the One beneath the cloud of the Many. For it is that central problem, as Chesterton saw more and more clearly throughout his life, that is the nexus of all philosophic confusion. Defending mysticism in 1908, he had drawn up, as we saw, a catalogue of errors connected only by their erroneousness; defending St. Thomas Aquinas in 1933, he calls multiplicity "this sharp and crooked corner" round which "all the sophists have followed each other while the great Schoolman went up the high road of experience and expansion."[14] *That,* as he came to see, was the great problem: the multiplicity of forms, the mutability of things.

We have said that there is an intuitive and a rational solution. In a sense the antithesis is false, because both depend on knowing where you are going before you start. The contemplative sees: the successful rationalist, guided by the instinct for being, sees imperfectly and secures himself with reason: he casts a thread across the abyss and follows it with a cable.

Lewis Carroll, as often, is ready with a parable:

Alice opened the door and found that it led into a small passage, not much larger than a rathole; she knelt down and looked along the passage into the loveliest garden you ever saw. How she longed to get out of that dark hall, and wander about among those beds of bright flowers and those cool fountains, but she could not even get her head through the doorway; "and even if my head *would* go through," thought poor Alice, "it would be of very little use without my shoulders. Oh, how I wish I could shut up like a telescope! I think I could, if I only knew how to begin."[15]

The problem of how to begin is for the rational philosopher the cogent problem; but the sterile rationalist is in an even sadder case than Alice: he has not even seen the garden. It would have delighted Chesterton, had the example occurred to him, that Alice first glimpsed it on her knees.

The glimpse of the garden is the intuition of being. The job of reason is to make the intuition explicit. Reason, like mysticism, will lead to the One if it starts with the right premise; which premise Plato felt rather than justified, but which the Schoolman in their great synthesis called Being, and justified as a starting-point by finding it naked in the first perceptions of a child.

Reason starting anywhere else, says Chesterton, will go astray; and casting into a strong epigram the mystic's tremendous sense that the things of the earth are vanity of vanities, he says that "Impressionism . . . puts what one notices before what one knows. It means the monstrous heresy that seeing is believing."[16]

So we begin with a paradox. Seeing is not believing, because what is seen changes constantly, and by its mutability has led all the philosophers astray. At the sight of change, he says, "many sages lose sight of the first principle of reality, which they would concede at first, and fall back on saying that there is nothing except change, or nothing except comparison, or nothing except flux; or in effect that there is nothing at all."[17]

That is madness: but "mysticism keeps men sane,"[18] because it incorporates the paradoxes of being. Reason, moving by definition in a straight line, misses the bend in the road: it goes wildly astray when it encounters the first paradox, which is the presence of diversity in likeness.[19]

Mysticism keeps men sane. As long as you have mystery you have health; when you destroy mystery you create morbidity. The ordinary man has always been sane, because the ordinary man has always been a mystic. He has permitted the twilight. He has always had one foot on earth and the other in fairyland. He has always left himself free to doubt his gods; but (unlike the agnostic of to-day) free also to believe in them. He has always cared more for truth than for consistency. If he saw two truths that seemed to contradict each other, he would take the two truths and the contradiction along with them. . . . Thus he has always believed that there was such a thing as fate, but such a thing as free will also. Thus he believed that children were indeed the kingdom of heaven, but nevertheless ought to be obedient to the kingdom of earth. He admired youth because it was young and age because it was not. It was exactly this balance of apparent contradictions that has been the whole buoyancy of the healthy man. The whole secret of mysticism is this: that man can understand everything by the help of what he does not understand. The morbid logician seems to make everything lucid, and succeeds in making everything mysterious. The mystic allows one thing to be mysterious, and everything else becomes lucid. The determinist makes the theory of causation quite clear, and finds that he cannot say "if you please" to the housemaid. The Christian permits free will to remain a sacred mystery; but because of this his relations with the housemaid become of a sparkling and crystal clearness. He puts the seed of dogma in a central darkness; but it branches forth in all directions with abounding natural health.[20]

Some five years earlier than *Orthodoxy*, in 1903-1904, he had gone over the same argument with different details in his controversy with the atheist Robert Blatchford in the *Clarion*. The passage begins *in medias res* with the ancient charge of paradox invented to startle:

> Some Determinists fancy that Christianity invented a dogma like Free Will for fun—a mere contradiction. This is absurd. You have the contradiction, whatever you are. Determinists tell me, with a degree of truth, that Determinism makes no difference to daily life. That means that although the Determinist knows men to have no free will, yet he goes on treating them as if they had.
>
> The difference, then, is very simple. The Christian puts the contradiction into his philosophy. The Determinist puts it into his daily habits. The Christian states as an avowed mystery what the Determinist calls nonsense. The Determinist has the same nonsense for breakfast, dinner, tea, and supper every day of his life. . . .
>
> All the straight roads of logic lead to some Bedlam, to Anarchism or to passive obedience, to treating the universe as a clockwork of matter or else as a delusion of the mind. It is only the Mystic, the man who accepts the contradictions, who can laugh and walk easily through the world.
>
> Are you surprised that the same civilization which believed in the Trinity discovered steam?[21]

I have reserved midway through the argument a sentence which so echoes another key sentence of thirty years later as to exhibit the astonishing consistency of his thought, the innumerable particular perceptions harmonizing in his vast metaphysical intuition. He had never to search for examples any more than a man with eyes has to search for examples of colour. For he had flung at Blatchford in exultation the claim that "Mystery by its darkness enlightens all things. Once grant him that, and life is life, and bread is bread, and cheese is cheese. He can laugh and fight."[22] Thirty years later he finds the philosophy of St. Thomas "founded on the universal common conviction that eggs are eggs."

The Hegelian may say that an egg is really a hen, because it is part of an endless process of Becoming; the Berkeleian may hold that poached eggs only exist as a dream exists; since it is quite as easy to call the dream the cause of the eggs as the eggs the cause of the dream; the Pragmatist may believe that we get the best out of scrambled eggs by forgetting that they ever were eggs, and only remembering the scramble. But no pupil of St. Thomas needs to addle his brains in order to addle his eggs; to put his head at any peculiar angle in looking at eggs, or squinting at eggs, or winking the other eye in order to see a new simplification of eggs. The Thomist stands in the broad daylight of the brotherhood of men, in their common consciousness that eggs are not hens or dreams or mere practical assumptions; but things attested by the authority of the Senses, which is from God.[23]

The beginning of the metaphysical vision, then, is to see things: to see, and to see *things*, and accept them with their inherent mystery: which process may roughly be called seeing them with surprise. The crude, believe-it-or-not connotations of this phrase, prompted, it must be admitted, by Chesterton's spurious Toby-jug heartiness, have led many a critic away from his profundity. His real concern is with a metaphysical art of wonder which he calls "the life of men and the beginning of the praise of God."[24] That is the beginning, and the refusal of humankind to be surprised—that is, to be aware— is the primary problem for him who would communicate his vision. In the *Autobiography* Chesterton tells a parable:

When I was a young journalist on the *Daily News*, I wrote in some article or other the sentence, "Clapham, like every other city, is built on a volcano." . . . My immediate superior . . . glowered at me in a heavy resentful manner. . . .

"But I was glorifying Clapham!" I cried pathetically, "I was showing it as epical and elemental and founded in the holy flame." "You think you're funny, don't you?" he said. "I think I'm right," I said, making the modest claim not for the last time; and then, not for the last but perhaps for the first time, the terrible truth dawned on me.

. . . The citizen of Clapham *could* not believe that I meant what I said. . . . He could not even say the word so that the first syllable of "Clapham" sounded like the last syllable of "thunderclap." There was utterly veiled from his sight the visionary Clapham, the volcanic Clapham, what I may be allowed to put upon the cosmic map as Thunderclapham.

The Clapham journalist, who glowered at me, has been the problem of my life. . . . Everything that I have thought and done grew originally out of that problem which seemed to me a paradox. . . . This was the primary problem for me, certainly in order of time and largely in order of logic. It was the problem of how men could be made to realize the wonder and splendour of being alive, in environments which their own daily criticism treated as dead-alive, and which their imagination had left for dead. It is normal for a man to boast if he can, or even when he can't, that he is a citizen of no mean city. But these men had really resigned themselves to being citizens of mean cities, stretched away far beyond the horizon; mean in architecture, mean in costume, mean even in manners; but, what was the only thing that really mattered, mean in the imaginative conception of their own inhabitants. . . . The modern way of life, only professing to be prosaic, pressed upon them day and night and was the real moulder of their minds.[25]

Two pages later the argument becomes more personal and more promising:

My madness, which was considerable, was wholly within. But that madness was more and more moving in the direction of some vague and visionary revolt against the prosaic flatness of a nineteenth-century city and civilization; an imaginative impatience with the cylindrical hats and rectangular houses; in short, that movement of the mind I have already associated with Napoleon of Notting Hill and the impatient patriot of Clapham. I had perhaps got no further than the feeling that those imprisoned in these inhuman outlines were human beings: that it was a bad thing that living souls should be thus feebly and crudely represented by houses like ill-drawn diagrams of Euclid, or streets and railways like dingy sections of machinery. . . .

I never doubted that the human beings inside the houses were themselves almost miraculous; like magic and talismanic dolls, in whatever ugly dolls'-houses.

For me, those brown brick boxes were really Christmas boxes. For, after all, Christmas boxes often came tied up in brown paper; and the jerrybuilders' achievements in brown brick were often extremely like brown paper.[26]

At the time when this vision was dawning, he put it even more concisely:

To the child, the tree and the lamp-post are . . . both supernatural. For both are splendid and unexplained. The flower with which God crowns the one, and the flame with which Sam the lamplighter crowns the other, are equally the gold of fairy-tales. In the middle of the wildest fields, the most rustic child is, ten to one, playing at steam-engines. And the only spiritual or philosophic objection to steam-engines . . . is that men do not play at them. The evil is that the childish poetry of clock-work does not remain. The wrong is not that engines are too much admired, but that they are not admired enough. The sin is not that engines are mechanical, but that men are mechanical.[27]

Throughout his works, especially his earlier works, Chesterton insists repeatedly and frantically on the poetry of things. In *The Napoleon of Notting Hill*, men in frockcoats become dragons walking backwards,[28] clouds a load of waters, beneath which "men move like fishes, feeling that they are on the floor of a sea."[29] In *Tremendous Trifles* trees in the wind are "straining and tearing and lashing as if they were a tribe of dragons each tied by the tail,"[30] and a railway station, like a cathedral, has "ritual . . .

dedicated to the celebration of water and fire, the two prime elements of all human ceremonial."[31] Adam Wayne, the earliest of the red-haired Chestertonian heroes innocently and unconsciously imbued with the Chestertonian vision,[32] appeals in ironic innocence of prosaic commerce to the grocer's peril from a too-cosmopolitan philosophy:

"I can imagine what it must be to sit all day as you do surrounded with wares from all the ends of the earth, from strange seas that we have never sailed and strange forests that we could not even picture. No eastern king ever had such argosies or such cargoes coming from the sunrise and the sunset, and Solomon in all his glory was not enriched like one of you. India is at your elbow," he cried, lifting his voice and pointing his stick at a drawer of rice, the grocer making a movement of some alarm, "China is before you, Demerara is behind you, America is above your head, and at this very moment, like some old Spanish admiral, you hold Tunis in your hands." . . .

The grocer sat for some little while, with dim eyes and his mouth open, looking rather like a fish. Then he scratched the back of his head and said nothing. Then he said,

"Anything out of the shop, sir?"[33]

Twenty years later we meet the same grocer transformed by the Revolution of Notting Hill, moulded now nearer to the heart's desire of Adam Wayne and, as he realizes, of his own secret self:

He was dressed in a long and richly embroidered robe of blue, brown, and crimson, interwoven with an Eastern complexity of pattern, and covered with obscure symbols and pictures, representing his wares passing from hand to hand and from nation to nation. Round his neck was the chain with the Blue Argosy cut in turquoise, which he wore as Grand Master of the Grocers. The whole shop had the sombre and sumptuous look of its owner. . . . The tea was stored in great blue and green vases, inscribed with the nine indispensable sayings of the wise men of China. Other vases of a confused orange and purple, less rigid and dominant, more humble and dreamy, stored symbolically the tea of India. A row of caskets of a simple silvery metal contained tinned meats. Each was wrought with some rude rhythmic form, as a shell, a horn, a fish, or an apple, to indicate what material had been canned in it.[34]

And recalling his enlightenment, he muses:

"I thought nothing of being a grocer then . . . isn't that mad enough for anybody? I thought nothing of all the wonderful places that my goods come from, and wonderful ways that they are made. I did not know that I was for all practical purposes a king with slaves spearing fishes near the secret pool and gathering fruit in the islands under the world. My mind was blank on the thing. I was as mad as a hatter."[35]

Chesterton's audience in 1904 would have thought the new and not the old grocer mad as a hatter; wherein lay the superficial, rhetorical paradox. But it was precisely the enlightenment of Mr. Mead the grocer that the author wished, quite simply and sincerely, to produce in every reader. "I deny most energetically," he said, "that anything is or can be uninteresting";[36] and by every device of headlong metaphor and gorgeous imagery he sought to reveal the thrill of the commonplace: he sought to encourage a healthy Wonder.

In an essay "On Telegraph Poles" he sees Nature herself rearing up tree after tree with "a weird rhythm in this very repetition . . . as if the earth were resolved to repeat a single shape until the shape shall turn terrible." He goes on:

Have you ever tried the experiment of saying some plain word, such as "dog," thirty times? By the thirtieth time it has become a word like "snark" or "pobble." It does not become tame, it becomes wild, by repetition. In the end a dog walks about as startling and undecipherable as Leviathan or Croquemitaine.

It may be that this explains the repetitions in Nature; it may be for this reason that there are so many leaves and pebbles. Perhaps they are not repeated so that they may grow familiar. Perhaps they are repeated only in the hope that they may at last grow unfamiliar. Perhaps a man is not startled at the first cat he sees, but jumps into the air with surprise at the seventy-ninth cat. Perhaps he has to pass through thousands of pine trees before he finds the one that is really a pine tree.[37]

"One elephant having a trunk was odd," he remarks in *Orthodoxy*, "but all elephants having trunks looked like a plot."[38] The next step was obviously to seek out the Plotter.

It is, or should be, plain at this point how wonder leads logically to gratitude and so to God; but the

argument as Chesterton developed it in maturer
years takes a turn of uncommon subtlety, that en-
sures its retaining metaphysical relevance. There is,
of course, really no argument present, but rather
the articulation of an immediate vision; to speak
as we have just spoken is simply to enforce in yet
another way the essential truth that Chesterton's
wonder is intrinsically metaphysical and not forced.
It bears only a superficial resemblance to that
aroused by the journalist who set the world on its
ear some years ago with the claim that Lindbergh
was the sixty-seventh to fly the Atlantic: a truth at
which he had arrived by totalling the passengers in
two dirigibles and a seaplane. The reader will not
find in Chesterton anything so profitless as that kind
of gaping. His wonder is directed not towards mathematical accidents like two-headed calves, but at
things in their analogical existence. Not that he did
not skirt that peril. One might say that Chesterton,
as enlightenment dawned, withdrew gradually from
a perilous dance on the brink of reading thoughts
into things, and came to concentrate on their "thing-
ness." It was inevitable from the sheer exigencies of
vocabulary that he should have risked this descent:
for if people are not going to get properly excited
about hansom cabs unless you present them as one-
eyed dragons, you are in danger yourself, through
mere missionary habit, of coming to think that their

excitement consists in their resemblance to dragons. You are apt to find things exciting because of what you can read into them.

An early essay, "What I Found in My Pocket," reveals Chesterton in this fashion pleasing himself with arabesques of his own invention:

The next thing that I took out was a pocket-knife. A pocket-knife, I need hardly say, would require a thick book of moral meditations all to itself. A knife typifies one of the most primary of those practical origins upon which as upon low, thick pillars all our human civilization reposes. Metals, the mystery of the thing called iron and of the thing called steel, led me off half-dazed into a kind of dream. I saw into the entrails of dim, damp woods: where the first man, among all the common stones, found the strange stone. I saw a vague and violent battle, in which stone axes broke and stone knives were splintered against something shining and new in the hands of one desperate man. I heard all the hammers upon all the anvils of the earth. I saw all the swords of feudal and all the wheels of industrial war. For the knife is only a secret sword. I opened it and looked at that brilliant and terrible tongue which we call a blade; and I thought that perhaps it was a symbol of the oldest of the needs of man.[39]

"Moral meditations" . . . "I thought it was the symbol" . . . the pleasure is splendid but, so to speak, impure. Far nearer to the primary joy in things is the catalogue of smells in "The Song of Quoodle," written twenty years later:

The brilliant smell of water,
The brave smell of a stone,
The smell of dew and thunder,
And old bones buried under . . .

The wind from winter forests,
The scent of scentless flowers,
The breath of bride's adorning,
The smell of snare and warning,
The smell of Sunday morning,
God gave to us for ours.[40]

Nearly contemporary with "The Song of Quoodle" is an essay defining the heresy of reading the wonderful qualities into things:

When (our contemporary mystics) said that a wooden post was wonderful . . . they meant that they could make something wonderful out of it by thinking about it. "Dream, there is no truth," said Mr. Yeats, "but in your own heart." The modern mystic looked for the post, not outside in the garden, but inside, in the mirror of his own mind. But the mind of the mystic, like a dandy's dressing-room, was entirely made of mirrors. That glass repeated glass like doors opening inwards for ever; till one could hardly see that inmost chamber of unreality where the post made its last appearance. And as the mirrors of the modern mystic's mind are most of them curved and many of them cracked, the post in its ultimate reflection looked like all sorts of things; a waterspout, the tree of knowledge, a sea-serpent standing upright, a twisted column of the new natural architecture, and so on. . . . But I was never interested in mirrors; that is, I was never primarily interested in my own reflection—or reflections. I am interested in wooden posts, which do startle me like miracles. I am interested in the post that stands waiting outside my door, to hit me over the head, like a giant's club in a fairy-tale. All my mental doors open outwards into a world I have not made. My last door of liberty opens upon a world of sun and solid things, of objective adventures. The post in the garden; the thing I could neither create nor expect; strong plain daylight on stiff upstanding wood: it is the Lord's doing and it is marvellous in our eyes.

"To me the post is wonderful because it is there; there whether I like it or not," he goes on; and concludes hinting desperately at "that strange and high indifference that belongs only to things that are."[41]

The post is wonderful because it is *there*: which is not the same thing as being wonderful because you can read wonders into it. Equally important, it is not the same thing as being wonderful because it has knots in it. Its Being is far more important in every sense than such superficial adornments to being as woodenness or knottiness. Chesterton saw from the very first that being is more wonderful than any of its individualities. "Man is something more awful than men; something more strange. The sense of the miracle of humanity itself should always be more vivid to us than any marvels of power, intellect, art, or civilization. . . . Death is more tragic even than death by starvation. Having a nose is more comic even than having a Norman nose."[42]

Commenting in the *Autobiography* on this clarification of vision, he describes his young self "all groping and groaning and travailing with an inchoate and half-baked philosophy of my own, which was very nearly the reverse of the remark that where there is nothing there is God. The truth presented itself to me, rather, in the form that where there is anything there is God. Neither statement is adequate in philosophy: but I should have been amazed to know how near in some ways was my Anything to the *Ens* of St. Thomas Aquinas."[43]

The *Ens* of St. Thomas Aquinas, the Thomist's very emphatic statement (with a blow on the table), "There *is* an Is,"[44] is thus the only sure passport to reality. Neglecting metaphysical wonder, we sin by regarding creation with presumption or with despair[45]; commencing with wonder but wondering in the wrong way, we are landed in the swamp of reading thoughts into things.

Neglecting wonder, we sin by regarding creation with presumption or with despair. That is the essence of the argument so far, as Chesterton finally summarized it in his final book, under the parable of the dandelion:

The only way to enjoy a weed is to feel unworthy even of a weed. Now there are two ways of complaining of the weed or the flower; and one was the fashion in my youth and the other is the fashion in my later days;

but they are not only both wrong, but both wrong
because the same thing is right. The pessimists of my
boyhood, when confronted with the dandelion, said
with Swinburne:

> "I am weary with days and hours
> Blown buds of barren flowers,
> Desires and dreams and powers
> And everything but sleep."

And at that I cursed them and kicked at them and
made an exhibition of myself; having made myself the
champion of the Lion's Tooth, with a dandelion ram-
pant on my crest. But there is a way of despising the
dandelion which is not that of the dreary pessimist, but
of the more offensive optimist . . . ultimately based on
the strange and staggering heresy that a human being
has a *right* to dandelions; that in some extraordinary
fashion we can demand the very pick of all the dandelions in the garden of Paradise; that we owe no thanks
for them at all, and need feel no wonder at them at all;
and above all no wonder at being thought worthy to
receive them. Instead of saying, like the old religious
poet, "What is man that Thou carest for him, or the
son of man that Thou regardest him?" we are to say . . .
like the bad-tempered Major in the club, "Is this a
chop fit for a gentleman?" Now I not only dislike this
attitude quite as much as the Swinburnian pessimistic
attitude, but I think it comes to very much the same
thing: to the actual loss of appetite for the chop or
the dish of dandelion-tea. And the name of it is Presumption and the name of its twin brother is Despair.[46]

On the brink of the ultimate conclusion of so
much thought, it is imperative to recall that we are
not, and Chesterton was not, rehearsing stages in

a proof: certainly not a proof of the existence of God. We are exhibiting a series of observations in the light of which it became natural and indeed habitual for Chesterton to see that all Being is in God; from which it is but a step to the logical and theological proposition that God sustains all Being. He saw, be it repeated, before he started to reason; and recorded not his reasonings but analogues of his visions. Hence the step from Things to the Creator is taken by him in any number of ways. The problem a thinking man sets out to solve is ultimately, as we have said, the problem of Unity in Multiplicity: of the way things vary though they are at one: by its very statement, a problem in analogy. And it was this perpetual consciousness of God as the one-ness of the universe, as a term, so to speak, in the analogy, that solved the problem for Chesterton perpetually. When we have gone two pages further with the argument it will be easy to see where the paradoxes come from, once God is admitted to every vision; but it is essential to remember that this argument is in the case of Chesterton logical and not historical; he saw the relevance of God from the beginning and knew where he was going before he got there. Hence the outburst of paradoxical expression at every stage, even in the contemplation of things as things with no apparent consciousness of their analogical meaning.

Well, then, enter God. Cecil Chesterton handily sums up the penultimate condition of his brother's vision:

Man cannot live by a philosophy which denies the existence of anything good behind the Universe. Such a philosophy leads to pessimism and despair. As little can he live by a philosophy which recognizes the visible Universe itself as divinity and exemplar—by Pantheism or Nature Worship. Such a philosophy leads to Anarchism and crime.[47]

We cannot repose in the Many, neither can we despair of the Many. It is inhuman not to press on to the One. Let Gilbert finish it—

The one leads logically to murder and the other to suicide. . . . Then comes a fantastic thing and says to us, "You are right to enjoy the birds, but wicked to copy them. There is a good thing behind all these things, yet all these things are lower than you. The Universe is right, but the world is wicked. The thing behind all is not cruel, like a bird, but good, like a man." And the wholesome thing in us says, "I have found the high road." . . . After an agony of thought the world found the safe path. . . . It was the Christian God. He made Nature, but He was Man.[48]

This logical step from the strange creation to its inconceivable begetter, from the Many to the One, from Being to All Being, is, significantly enough, present in the analogical perception unbuttressed by the revealed dogma of the Incarnation. The God of Israel who had not yet put on flesh comes in upon the Whirlwind of the Book of Job to establish the Chestertonian position out of His own mouth. In his *Introduction to the Book of Job,* Chesterton notes

> The fine inspiration by which God comes in at the end, not to answer riddles, but to propound them. . . . The mechanical optimist . . . points out that the fine thing about the world is that it can all be explained. That is the one point, if I may say so, on which God in return, is explicit to the point of violence. God says, in effect, that if there is one fine thing about the world, as far as men are concerned, it is that it cannot be explained. He insists upon the inexplicableness of everything: "Hath the rain a father? . . . Out of whose womb came the ice?" He goes farther, and insists on the positive and palpable unreason of things: "Hast thou sent the rain upon the desert where no man is, and upon the wilderness wherein there is no man?" God will make man see things, if it is only against the black background of nonentity. God will make Job see a startling universe if He can only do it by making Job see an idiotic universe. To startle man God becomes for an instant a blasphemer; one might almost say that God becomes for an instant an atheist. He unrolls before Job a long panorama of created things, the horse, the eagle, the raven, the wild ass, the peacock, the ostrich, the crocodile. He so describes each of them that it sounds like a monster walking in the sun. The whole is a sort of psalm or rhapsody of the sense of wonder. The maker of all things is astonished at the things He has Himself made.[49]

The paradox, the contradiction, the unreasonable thing, is God's message to man; it is even God's answer to the sceptic. "He turns rationalism against itself. He seems to say that if it comes to asking questions, He can ask some questions which will fling down and flatten out all conceivable human questioners."[50] On those questions, on their acceptance simply as questions and contradictions, is reared all perdurable faith. It was Mark of Rome in *The Ballad of the White Horse* whose shield could turn back the faery dart of Elf, gift of the watermaidens: Mark who

> . . . was come of the glittering towns
>   Where hot white details show,
> Where men can number and expound,
> And his faith grew in a hard ground
> Of doubt and reason and falsehood found,
>   Where no faith else could grow.
>
> Belief that grew of all beliefs
>   One moment back was blown
> And belief that stood on unbelief
>   Stood up iron and alone.[51]

The ultimate analogical vision of the incredible heart of things is responsible for paradoxes strewn up and down Chesterton's writings throughout his career:

(Blake) held that eternal innocence to be an actual and even awful thing. . . . If there were a lamb in one of Aesop's fables, Aesop would never be so silly as to represent him as angry. But Christianity is more daring than Aesop, and the wrath of the Lamb is one of its great paradoxes.[52]

* * *

Men who could hardly write had written up inscriptions; and somehow they were dogmas as well as jokes. . . . Somebody wrote, "God Bless Christ the King"; and I knew I was staring at one of the staggering paradoxes of Christianity.[53]

* * *

If we are to be truly gay, we must believe that there is some eternal gaiety in the nature of things. We cannot enjoy thoroughly even a *pas de quatre* at a subscription dance unless we believe that the stars are dancing to the same tune. Nobody can be really hilarious but the serious man. . . . Ultimately a man can enjoy nothing except the nature of things. Ultimately a man can enjoy nothing except religion.[54]

* * *

> The dreadful joy Thy Son has sent
>   Is heavier than any care;
> We find, as Cain his punishment,
>   Our pardon more than we can bear.[55]

* * *

> Wherein God's ponderous mercy hangs
> On all my sins and me,
> Because He does not take away
> The terror from the tree
> And stones still shine along the road
> That are and cannot be.[56]

* * *

"The things that cannot be and that are."[57] That is the starkest paradoxical statement of the analogical perception, the key to wonder, to gratitude, and to God. Being transcends reason, Being encloses contradictions. Being, thinks St. Thomas Aquinas and Chesterton after him, is intrinsically analogical.

It is on the strength of such passages that Chesterton has been loosely termed a "mystic." It should be plain by now that the analogical perceptions these paradoxes reflect and exploit is altogether different not in degree but in kind from the mode of supernatural experience that constitutes mysticism proper. Gerard Manley Hopkins has suffered from the same well-meant praise; in fact, however, Hopkins' perception is analogical and not at all unlike Chesterton's, the difference between his poetry and Chesterton's rhetoric being that the mode of organization in a Hopkins poem *is* poetic: that is, dramatic and intensely felt. Chesterton never achieves a great poem because his poems are compilations of statements not intensely felt but only intensely meant. This is not to say that he is less sincere than Hopkins; it is rather to say that the vision came so easily, with so little struggle, and inspired so great a confidence, that he could realize no real personal conflict centering on it. One can perceive the case at its crudest by reflecting that Chesterton never underwent the kind of experience of self-distrust that issued in Hopkins' "terrible sonnets." There is a sense in which it is to his praise that he could not be a poet.

We cannot here go into the resemblance between Chesterton's perception and Hopkins'. We can however demonstrate that the mode in which the perception is realized is philosophical rather than poetic by examining his treatment of the Incarnation. It is plainly an exegetical treatment: an exploration of the implications of the fact: an exploration, not a concentration. It is wholly in the tradition of Christian exegetical paradox that reaches down through sermons from the time of the Fathers.

Be it repeated, there is no implication here that he did not mean intensely and contemplate continually. The paradox of the dying God gains greater and greater intensity for him throughout his life, until ultimately it occupies the centre of his thought as the central mystery of the relation of God to man, and the mainspring of all right human conduct.

"After an agony of thought," Chesterton had cried against Blatchford at the beginning of his controversial career, "after an agony of thought the world found the sane path. . . . It was the Christian God. He made Nature, but He was Man."[58] The ancient gulf which inhibits the ordinary imagination, the gulf between God and His chief creature, the gulf which has betrayed so many into denying God or belittling Man, was, Chesterton repeatedly tells us, bridged "when a strolling carpenter's apprentice said calmly and almost carelessly, like one looking over his shoulder: 'Before Abraham was, I am.' "[59]

Indeed the Incarnation altered the atmosphere even of rational philosophy, and permitted the mediaeval neo-Aristotelian appeal to the senses away from mere mystery:

There really was a new reason for regarding the senses, and the sensations of the body, with a reverence at which the great Aristotle would have stared, and no man in the ancient world could have begun to understand. The Body was no longer what it was when Plato and Porphyry and the old mystics had left it for dead. It had hung upon a gibbet. It had risen from a tomb. It was no longer possible for the soul to despise the senses, which had been the organs of something that was more than man. Plato might despise the flesh: but God had not despised it. The senses had truly become sanctified; as they are blessed one by one at a Catholic baptism. "Seeing is believing" was no longer the platitude of a mere idiot, or common individual, as in Plato's world; it was mixed up with real conditions of real belief. Those revolving mirrors that send messages to the brain of man, that light that breaks upon the brain, these had truly revealed to God himself the path to Bethany or the light on the high rock of Jerusalem. These ears that resound with common noises had reported also to the secret knowledge of God the noise of the crowd that strewed palms and the crowd that cried for the Crucifixion. After the Incarnation had become the idea that is central in our civilization, it was inevitable that there should be a return to materialism, in the sense of the serious value of matter and the making of the body. When once Christ had risen, it was inevitable that Aristotle should rise again.[60]

Brilliantly as this is put, its substance is wholly traditional, and it is to be found among the Fathers and ante-Nicene writers *passim*. Tertullian's entire treatise *De Carne Christi* is devoted to the point. It is scarcely necessary to add that Chesterton relied on no such prompting from traditional sources, though he had almost certainly run across some of them. He arrived at his exegesis in the same way as the Fathers themselves: by philosophical scrutiny.

This is equally true of the chapter in *The Everlasting Man* which dwells on the repeated paradoxes of the Incarnation of God in Jesus Christ.[61] Divine, like human, history begins in a cave, "in a cellar under the very floor of the world," and in a paragraph that reverberates with overtones of God's great challenge to Job, "Where wast thou when I laid the foundations of the earth?", we are told how

In that second creation there was indeed something symbolical in the roots of the primeval rock or the horns of the prehistoric herd. God also was a Cave-Man, and had also traced strange shapes of creatures, curiously coloured, upon the wall of the world; but the pictures that he made had come to life.

A mass of legend and literature, which increases and will never end, has repeated and rung the changes on that single paradox; that the hands that had made the sun and stars were too small to reach the huge heads of the cattle. Upon this paradox, we might almost say upon this jest, all the literature of our faith is founded. . . . Any agnostic or atheist whose childhood has ever known a real Christmas has ever afterwards, whether he likes it or not, an association in his mind between two ideas that most of mankind must regard as remote from each other: the idea of a baby and the idea of an unknown strength that sustains the stars.[62]

This sort of stimulating statement of the implications of that central event is carried on in the same way in dozens of different directions, so that the Incarnation is shown to give meaning to an incredible amount of material. The baby in the cave, for example, is the type of that love of small things which is so prominent a part of Chesterton's philosophy: the love of small nations[63], of toy theatres[64], of pocket-knives and cottages and lumps of clay[65]:

It might be suggested in a somewhat violent image, that nothing had happened in that fold or crack in the great grey hills except that the whole universe had been turned inside out. I mean that all the eyes of wonder and worship which had been turned outwards to the largest thing were now turned inwards to the smallest. . . . God who had been only a circumference was seen as a centre; and a centre is infinitely small.[66]

The wise man will follow a star, low and large and fierce in the heavens; but the nearer he comes to it the smaller and smaller it grows, till he finds it in the humble lantern over some little inn or stable. Not till we know the high things shall we know how lowly they are.[67]

The small things are intrinsically divine, as that baby was divine: because that baby was divine. Since that birth, Alfred can rejoice in his tiny kingdom as Mary the human Queen of Heaven rejoices in the tiny earth:

"Alfred in his orchard among apples green and red" saw as in a vision

> An island like a little book
>   Full of a hundred tales,
> Like the gilt page the good monks pen,
> That is all smaller than a wren,
> Yet hath high towns, meteors, and men
>   And suns and spouting whales.
>
> A land having a light on it
>   In the river dark and fast
> An isle with utter clearness lit
> Because a saint has stood in it
> Where flowers are flowers indeed and fit
>   And trees are trees at last.[68]

While among "Our Lady's Trinkets" there are enumerated, in a similar catalogue of created things,

> The standing whirlpool of the stars,
> The wheel of all the world,
> Is a ring for Our Lady's finger
> With the suns and moons empearled.
> With stars for stones to please her
> Who sits playing with her rings
> With the great heart that a woman has
> And the love of little things.[69]

A brief inspection of the three excerpts above will show how the paradox by which a kingdom and a cosmos can be described as "little things" issues from an analogical vision that perceives all the essential relations simultaneously, and is rooted and made humanly relevant by the fact of the Incarnation.

Indeed, the Incarnation can be said to bring every strand of Chesterton's perception to a focus. That pugnacity, to take another example, which has gained him the title of the Last of the Crusaders[79], the pugnacity which animates the best of his otherwise formless verse, which appears in *The Napoleon of Notting Hill* as the war of the townsmen against the superstate, in *The Man Who Was Thursday* as the struggle of civilization against anarchy, in the Father Brown stories as the eternal conflict of sanity against the false philosophers, and which is reducible to the ultimately identical forms of particularity withstanding the attrition of chaos and truth withstanding the inroads of the Enemy, that pugnacity which remained from the first battle with Blatchford both a Chestertonian dynamic and a Chestertonian theme, is likewise prefigured for him in the Incarnation: for God was born "like an outcast or even an outlaw"[71] and the highest thing could henceforth "only work from below," something despised and yet something feared.

Olympus still occupied the sky like a motionless cloud moulded into many mighty forms; philosophy still sat in the high places and even on the thrones of kings, when Christ was born in the cave and Christianity in the catacombs.

. . . The early Church was important while it was still insignificant, and certainly while it was still impotent. It was important solely because it was intolerable; and in that sense it is true to say that it was intolerable because it was intolerant. It was resented because, in its own still and almost secret way, it had declared war. It had risen out of the ground to wreck the heaven and earth of heathenism.[72]

The principle of paradox we have seen to be contradiction, and it is not hard to see the relationship of contradiction to combat. Chesterton's fine justification of holy wars, adequately dramatized in *The Man Who Was Thursday,* contains both the principle of paradox and the way to truth: which principle is prefigured in the birth of Christ:

I sometimes think that when the two swords clash they are only the two blades of the shears of Fate: perhaps each blade of a pair of scissors fancies it is fighting the other to the death; but in truth they are in a greater hand, used together to a single end.[73]

So it is with the war between the two halves of a paradox; so it was with the war between the imperfect Christians and the still more imperfect philosophers, heretics, and kings; so it was with the Christ who brought not peace but a sword, yet came not to destroy but to save.

The Incarnation, because it focusses such diverse realities, is central not only for Chesterton but for the purposes of his expositor. Let us pursue one more train of examples. We have said that God's act in becoming a man renewed the human divinity of unfallen Eden; in that sense the Creation and the Redemption are one action, combining to secure the place of man himself as one of the generic paradoxes. Man being by his very nature infinitely less than God, his perfection, could he even achieve his perfection, would, as the principle of analogy shows, be infinitely less than that of God. Hence man's littleness, which is not achieved but only intensified by his sins. Yet man was created in the divine image, and God saw fit to assume the human image; hence man's surpassing dignity, with which his littleness makes intrinsic war. Man is a walking paradox, contingent and yet divine; his Fall by underlining his littleness contrasts with the Incarnation which underlines his greatness to make him more paradoxical still.[74]

Throughout Chesterton's work, the symbol of that central paradox, which Eden established and the Incarnation restored, is laughter: for laughter is the sign of an incongruity perceived. This truth puts Chesterton's own jokes in a surprising new light; it also lends relevance to the following remarks on humour:

Why is it funny that a man should sit down suddenly in the street? There is only one possible or intelligent reason: that man is the image of God. It is not funny that anything else should fall down: only that a man should fall down. No one sees a delicate absurdity in a stone falling down. No one stops in the road and roars with laughter at the sight of the snow coming down. The fall of thunderbolts is treated with some gravity. The fall of roofs and high buildings is taken seriously. It is only when a man tumbles down that we laugh. Why do we laugh? Because it is a grave religious matter. It is the fall of man. Only man can be absurd, for only man can be dignified.[75]

In *All Things Considered* he expresses through the same symbol of laughter another facet of the same paradox:

All the jokes about men sitting down on their hats are really theological jokes: they are concerned with the Dual Nature of Man. They refer to the primary paradox that man is superior to all the things around him and yet is at their mercy.

Quite equally spiritual and subtle is the idea at the back of laughing at foreigners. It concerns the almost torturing truth of a thing being like oneself and yet not like oneself. Nobody laughs at what is entirely foreign; nobody laughs at a palm tree. But it is funny to see the familiar image of God disguised behind the black beard of a Frenchman or the black face of a negro.[76]

All genuine knowledge about man, all appreciation of man, comes from a recognition of this paradox:

It is not seeing things as they are to think first of Briareus with a hundred hands, and then call every man a cripple for only having two. . . . When we really see men as they are, we do not criticize but worship, and very rightly. For a monster with mysterious eyes and miraculous thumbs, with strange dreams in his skull, and a queer tenderness for this place or that baby, is truly a wonderful and unnerving matter. . . . All genuine appreciation rests on a certain mystery of humility and almost of darkness.[77]

And again,

The thing which is valuable and lovable in our eyes is man—the old beer-drinking, creed-making, fighting, failing, sensual, respectable man. And the things which have been founded on this creature immortally remain. . . . Christ . . . chose . . . a shuffler, a snob, a coward—in a word, a man. And upon this rock He has built His Church, and the gates of Hell have not prevailed against it.[78]

On this premise he attacks the scientific pretense that anthropomorphism is a process of making things more comfortable by giving them human attributes:

So long as a tree is a tree, it does not frighten us at all. It begins to be something alien, to be something strange, only when it looks like ourselves. When a tree really looks like a man, our knees knock under us. And when the whole universe looks like a man, we fall on our faces.[79]

Because man is paradoxical, he is comforted only by paradoxes; every suffering man repeats the suffering of God, and it is enough to remind him of this without seeking to explain it:

Job is not told that his misfortunes were due to his sins, or a part of any plan for his improvement. But in the prologue we see Job tormented not because he was the worst of men but because he was the best. It is the lesson of the whole work that man is most comforted by paradoxes. Here is the very darkest and strangest of the paradoxes; and it is by all human testimony the most reassuring. I need not suggest what a high and strange history awaited this paradox of the best man in the worst fortune. I need not say that in the freest and most philosophical sense there is one Old Testament figure who is truly a type; or say what is pre-figured in the wounds of Job.[80]

There is a fine suggestion earlier in the same essay of the root of paradoxical speech in the need for hinting at that which the mind cannot grasp:

Job was comfortless before the speech of Jehovah and is comforted after it. He has been told nothing, but he feels the terrible and tingling atmosphere of something which is too good to be told. The refusal of God to explain His design is itself a burning hint of His design. The riddles of God are more satisfying than the solutions of men.[81]

Man is comforted by paradoxes because they remind him of his dignity.

The dignity of man is likewise at the root of Chesterton's sociology, and so of his multifarious polemic against the Servile State which would maintain the poor secure in factories. This he contrasts with the state of divided property which would restore to each small owner the essential dignity of a servant of God who controls in his own right a portion of the work of God, and in that practical sense, as elsewhere in a metaphysical sense, repeats the attitudes and preoccupations of his Creator. Chesterton sees "property as a natural right of men and not a legal privilege of lucky men; economics as the servant of ethics; the servant of the servant of God."[82]

It is also the phenomenon of a little man remembering his greatness that gives stuff to Chesterton's astonishingly recurrent metaphor of homesickness at home. When he was only twenty-two he first told the tale of the man who took "the shortest journey from one place to the same place," which is around the world[83]. Innocent Smith in *Manalive* was likewise to make that journey[84], and the battlers of *The Ball and the Cross* were to discover England under the impression that it was an unknown island[85], like the man who is presented in the introduction to *Orthodoxy* as the parable of Chesterton's own discovery of a truth nineteen hundred years old under the impression that it was a heresy of his own.[86] Continually the image recurs. It opens *The Everlasting Man*[87], it crops up in a discussion of Rhyme ("While all forms of genuine verse recur, there is in rhyme a sense of return to exactly the same place. . . . Rhythm deals with similarity, but rhyme with identity. Now in the one word identity are involved perhaps the deepest and certainly the dearest human things")[88]; it permeates and climaxes an essay on "Milton and Merry England"[89], and another on "The Riddle of the Ivy"[90]. And while in most of its manifestations it is superficially a recommendation to come back to things after an absence and see them with proper humility, it is equally, and hauntingly, a parable of man recalling his divinity but exiled from Eden. In this parable the very sense of wonder at things, from which we started, becomes identified with that memory of an earlier destiny among diviner things, with which the logical sequence closes.

The Incarnation reinforcing the dual nature of man gives rise also to a whole set of ethical paradoxes, since the indigestible paradox of man's greatness and littleness gives rise to a clash of concomitant emotions, pride and humility. That clash of virtues is but the type of many other clashing virtues: pomp and austerity, joy and resignation, love of life and indifference to it, love of the sinner and hatred of the sin—all of them fruits of contrasting and simultaneously operative functions of man.

The heart of Christian ethics, says Chesterton, is like the heart of paradox: not the mere dilution of one thing by its contrary, but their separation and exaggeration.

The average pagan, like the average agnostic, would merely say that he was content with himself, but not insolently self-satisfied, that there were many better and many worse, that his deserts were limited, but he would see that he got them. This . . . manly and rational position . . . being a mixture of two things, is a dilution of two things; neither is present in its full strength nor contributes its full colour. . . . It loses both the poetry of being proud and the poetry of being humble.

Christianity . . . separated the two ideas and then exaggerated them both. In one way Man was to be haughtier than he had ever been before; in another way he was to be humbler than he had ever been before. In so far as I am Man I am the chief of creatures. In so far as I am *a* man I am the chief of sinners. . . . Christianity thus held a thought of the dignity of man that could only be expressed in crowns rayed like the sun and fans of peacock plumage. Yet at the same time it could hold a thought about the abject smallness of man that could only be expressed in fasting and fantastic submission, in the grey ashes of St. Dominic and the white snows of St. Bernard.[91]

Paradox is the heart of Being; it is the heart of Man; it is the heart of Ethics. And all these paradoxes, as this long demonstration has shown, are facets of one simultaneous perception focused in one timeless event. All the pages from which I have quoted, and all the hundreds of pages like them, represent explorations of a single truth.

All that rests on the Incarnation. But to give a faithful account of Chesterton's thought we must add a coda exploring some of the same themes with reference to the Crucifixion. As far as he betrays any shift of interest at all it is simply a shift from the birth to the death of Christ. The Crucifixion fascinated him more and more as he grew older, though it is very early present in his thought. The central paradox of the life of Christ, Chesterton tells us, and ultimately the parent paradox of paradoxical man, is that God once died. The tragedy hanging over the life of man is that he is to die and knows that he is to die[92]; the contrary which balances that tragedy and makes it into a paradox, a tension of opposites and therefore a focus of life, is that God also once died, having also known that He would surely die. Death is the doom of man; death was the bride of Christ.[93]

The spectacle of a God dying is much more grandiose than the spectacle of a man living forever. The former suggests the awful changes that have really entered the alchemy of the universe; the latter is only vaguely reminiscent of hygienic octogenarians and Eno's Fruit Salts.[94]

It is the final demonstration of human dignity, that the Fall of Man could only be put right by the Fall of God: both of them acts of the will. In *The Ball and the Cross*, the atheist Turnbull says savagely,

"At least, it was your Jesus Christ who started all this bosh about being God."

For one instant MacIan opened the eyes of battle; then his tightened lips took a crooked smile and he said, quite calmly,

"No, the idea is older; it was Satan who first said that he was God."

"Then, what," asked Turnbull, very slowly, as he softly picked a flower, "what is the difference between Christ and Satan?"

"It is quite simple," replied the Highlander. "Christ descended into hell; Satan fell into it."

"Does it make such odds?" asked the freethinker.

"It makes all the odds," said the other. "One of them wanted to go up and went down; the other wanted to go down and went up. A god can be humble, a devil can only be humbled."[95]

In what is certainly one of his most ambitious poems, the "To St. Michael in Time of Peace" which *G. K.'s Weekly* published three months after Chesterton's death, the same contrast recurs:

When from the deeps a dying God astounded
Angels and devils who do all but die
Seeing Him fallen where thou couldst not follow,
Seeing Him mounted where thou couldst not fly,
Hand on the hilt, thou hast halted all thy legions
Waiting the *Tetelestai* and the acclaim
Swords that salute Him dead and everlasting
God beyond God and greater than His Name.

. . . They that come to quiet us, saying the sword is broken,
Break men with famine, fetter them with gold,
Sell them as sheep; and He shall know the selling
For he was more than murdered. He was sold.[96]

The Fall of God is the centre and the climax: the dying God slaying Himself with His own hand for the love of men. That is the central drama on which Chesterton insists, in the long tradition of Christian paradox, as the source of the duality of the world, so that everything is itself and yet the reflection of something more than itself; that is the source of the analogical duality of man, mighty enough to have been worth the death of God, mean enough to have doomed his God to die.

We have been led a long way from the philosophy that is the suicide of thought, and the reasonableness that is the end of reason. Chesterton's analogical perception of Being has led us from elementary wonder to the very heart of a paradoxical universe. It may be said without exaggeration that he ranks almost with St. Thomas himself in the comprehensiveness of that initial perception; and that very certainty and immediacy which makes it unnecessary for him to struggle at any time with any truth and so makes significant dramatic expression impossible for him places him securely not in the hierarchy of the artists but in one not less distinguished: the long line of exegetists and theologians who have successively explored the same cosmos in the light of the same vision, seeing all things ordered and all things mirroring greater and lesser things: the Fathers, philosophers, and Doctors of the Church.

VI: THE WORD AND THE WORLD

THE ESSENTIAL Chesterton is the man with the extraordinarily comprehensive intuition of being the implications of which we have been exploring. There is a sense in which his enormous literary production is a by-product; what must be praised in Chesterton is not the writing but the seeing. The reader who has followed the preceding chapters is well on the way to realizing this fact; if he has seen that Chesterton's wildest parallels and metaphors are not excogitated illustrations of the vision but ingredients of it he has gotten nearly all a commentary can give him. Our final task is to examine the nature and quality of Chesterton's writing, defining as we do so a third kind of paradox which may be labelled the aesthetic. It is essential to consider him as an artist, however inartistic he may be, because his vision is after all manifested in language, and his every excursion into language brings him up against certain problems of the artist.

We must first of all enforce a distinction that was

made in the opening pages of this book, between art as making in general and art as a significant expansion of sensibility. This may be most directly done by determining exactly what kind of merit can be claimed for Chesterton's poetry. Like most poets he is praised to-day by his admirers for the wrong reasons. Charity would suggest leaving the uncritical Chestertonian to his illusions, but prudence insists that the bubble must be pricked, because of the curiously exclusive nature of misguided praise. If a man is praised for the wrong reasons he will almost certainly not be praised for the right reasons. This is attested in the present instance by the abject refusal of Chestertonians to see that interest in their idol as a significant figure must centre not on his cleverness or heartiness but on his perceptivity.

Consider, for example, the opening of one of the best of Chesterton's poems, *Gloria in Profundis*:

> There has fallen on earth for a token
> A god too great for the sky.
> He has burst out of all things and broken
> The bounds of eternity:
> Into time and the terminal land
> He has strayed like a thief or a lover,
> For the wine of the world brims over,
> Its splendour is spilt on the sand.[1]

The paradoxes here are perhaps more directly and explicitly rooted in the Incarnation than any considered in the last chapter, and a little thought will justify any of them. Our concern here is with the mode of their poetic realization, and the judgment must be that the realization is not poetic at all, but intellectual. The alliteration (via Swinburne) and the hearty rhythmic thump (via Kipling) exert a hypnotic influence in their own right and direct attention *away from* the intellectual content. There is no development of imagery: one must pause, shutting one's ears to the sound, to think out the aptness of the thief, the lover, and the wine-cup as analogues for Christ; and each image exists in isolation, without connections before and after. The latter is also true of each stanza; the four stanzas of the poem may be arranged, without serious confusion, in any one of twenty-four possible orders. In sum, the reader is confronted with a cluster of epigrams while a brass band drums at his ears.

The reader who will compare this poem, or any Chesterton poem he likes, with, say, the fourth part of T. S. Eliot's "East Coker" (in *Four Quartets*) will have no difficulty perceiving the radical difference. Eliot, for example, writes, in a passage equally replete with paradox:

The whole earth is our hospital
Endowed by the ruined millionaire,
Wherein, if we do well, we shall
Die of the absolute paternal care
That will not leave us, but prevents us everywhere.[2]

Here the operative word is "die," finely enforced by its initial position in the line. Expectancy of the rhyme with "hospital" slows down the reading of "we shall"—a process accentuated by the parenthetical interruption "if we do well"—and further isolates the key-word "die," enforcing the paradoxical contrast with "doing well"; which contrast in turn suddenly expands the convalescent associations of "if we do well" to a moral well-doing implicated in the moral irony of the nature of man. These hints on the way one word in the stanza is made to function could be carried on indefinitely to involve all the rest of the poem, although written analysis is at best a clumsy demonstrative instrument. Enough has been said, however, to show that in the Eliot stanza all the poetic devices are enlisted behind, and not at cross-purposes with, the "meaning"; which meaning is not a detachable intellectual thing but consists in one's total response to the entire stanza.

This radical difference in the mode of working of the two poets cannot be brushed aside by calling the demonstrable differences merely finicky or ascribing Eliot's superiority to more laborious craftsmanship. Indeed the latter argument tells exactly the other way. Chesterton is simply uninterested in the job a serious poet undertakes. The merit that can be claimed for his verse, once the careful reader has shut his ears to the sound-effects and deciphered the relevance of the array of images, is simply the merit owing to any triumphal celebration. Read in this way, as celebrations of cosmic fact, his poems take on their full meaning; but it is a philosophical, not a poetical meaning, and a noisy rather than a perceptive celebration.

That he should write in this way is the inevitable consequence of the way he perceived. The conflicts reflected in the language are not in his mind but out in front of him, in the things; he admires them, he does not feel involved in them. His analogical vision was both total and in an odd way painless. It unfits him for poetry; it equips him admirably and beyond question for philosophy and exposition.

The next thing to be said about Chesterton as an artist is that his poetic failure carries with it no moral imputation. He fails because he is so constituted that certain gears will never mesh: not because he misconceives the moral basis of making. In a moral sense, in fact, and within the limits of a less intense definition that includes under "art" all making, even the making of expositions, he is unsurpassed in his time. He never fumbles to reach a position, because he never needs to reach a position. He occupies a central position all the time. And he never fumbles in stating some truth drawn from contemplation of the nature of things, because his statements are so intimately bound up with his perceptions that the central clarity of the latter induces an authoritative finality in the former. It cannot be too often repeated that his gifts and habits were such as to fit him pre-eminently for philosophical discourse. In a better age, with greater incentive for scholarship and less pressure for immediate, continuous, and dissipating journalistic action, he might have been a principal ornament of the mediaeval Sorbonne. It is doing him the fullest possible homage to call him a splendid anachronism: the operative word is splendid.

Yet he was by no means an anachronism in any moral or political sense. Indeed it is curious to compare his continual centrality with the centre to which the most recent of the intelligent socially conscious are turning. The comparison emphasizes even further Chesterton's firm roots in a timeless philosophy. For the post-war world is cluttered with the hulks of disillusioned Marxists, and some few of them are suddenly and earnestly discovering the kind of cultural conditions and the kind of conception of man which Chesterton had been celebrating since the turn of the century.

From a September, 1946 speech by André Malraux, for example, I extract the following numbed recognition that the nineteenth-century progressive dream that nourished Marxism is at last pragmatically dead:

At the end of the Nineteenth Century the voice of Nietzsche took up the classical refrain, "God is dead," and gave it a new and tragic sense. Everyone knew that the death of the deity meant the liberation and deification of man.

The question which faces us all to-day on this old European earth is whether not God but man is dead. . . .

Europe, ravaged and bloody, is not more ravaged and bloody than the picture of mankind which in the pre-war days it hoped to create.[3]

It is with pardonable satisfaction that one now turns to *Heretics*:

The modern man says, "Let us leave all these arbitrary standards and embrace liberty." This is, logically rendered, "Let us not decide what is good, but let it be considered good not to decide it." He says, "Away with your old moral formulae; I am for progress." This, logically stated, means, "Let us not settle what is good, but let us settle whether we are getting more of it." . . . Never perhaps since the beginning of the world has there been an age that had less right to use the word "progress" than we.[4]

Malraux is lamenting the passing on an ideal in which he had for a long time invested everything. Chesterton did not need to have any such ideal beaten out of his head by two bloody wars. *Heretics* was published in 1905.

The April, 1946 issue of *Politics*, to take another example, contains some 10,000 anxious words of socialist self-searching under the general title, "The Root is Man." The author is a sincere man, and a responsible one. Yet to follow him in his valiant, hesitant, fumbling approach to the Chestertonian position ("All I attempt here is to explain, as coherently as possible, why the Marxian approach to socialism no longer satisfies me, and to indicate the general direction in which I think a more fruitful approach may be made") is to realize most forcibly, while applauding a new political hopefulness, the fact that Mr. Dwight Macdonald is merely groping after the most elementary principles of *What's Wrong With the World*, which Chesterton dashed off in 1912. This is not to wish that Chesterton had been listened to long ago: too facile a mass conversion would have been unearned and subject to relapse. It is rather to wish that there had been, contemporary with him, twenty men of his unique gifts.

Such comparison of his spontaneity with the hampered and stammering effort of other men emphasizes the easy inevitability of phrase and analogue which made his vast output possible, and which is usually wrongly accounted for. What, to take a concrete instance, is the exact explanation of that Chestertonian habit which has so distressed so many sensitive reviewers, the habit of allowing a categorical conclusion to issue from a play upon words? Mr. Maurice Evans, for example, is concerned with

The illegitimate use to which Chesterton frequently puts his admirable command of word and image, so that proof appears, where, in fact, none exists. Analogy is obviously a very dangerous weapon in this respect, for what begins as an illustration may, after sufficient development, be accepted as proof. . . . For example, he observes that the American mentality is child-like and loves "to watch the wheels go round" (*Generally Speaking*). Then taking the metaphor literally, he argues from it: "watching the wheels go round" implies that they will return back to the same place, or if they move on, they will move in a rut. Therefore, Americans are conservative. This may be the case, but there is no logical connection in the argument.[5]

This may be the case, one must reply, but there is in fact no argument present. Mr. Evans does not realize that he has been told a parable.

The parable, as Belloc had the sagacity to observe, is Chesterton's chosen form:

His unique, his capital genius for illustration by parallel, by example, is his peculiar mark. . . . No one whatsoever that I can recall in the whole course of English letters had his amazing—I would almost say superhuman—capacity for parallelism.

Now parallelism is a gift or method of vast effect in the conveyance of truth.

Parallelism consists in the illustration of some unperceived truth by its exact consonance with the reflection of a truth already known and perceived. . . .

Thus if some ass propounds that a difference of application destroys the validity of a doctrine, or that particulars are the enemies of universals, Chesterton will answer: "It is as though you were to say that I cannot be an Englishman because I am a Londoner." . . .

Always, in whatever manner he launched the parallelism, he produced the shock of illumination. He *taught*.

He made men see what they had not seen before. He made them *know*. He was an architect of certitude, whenever he practised this art in which he excelled.

The example of the parable in Holy Writ will at once occur to the reader. It is of the same origin and of similar value. The "parable" of the Gospels differs only from pure parallelism in the artifice of introducing a story in order to capture the reader's mind. But in essence a parable is the same thing as a parallelism.

Let us remark in conclusion that parallelism is of particular value in a society such as ours which has lost the habit of thinking. It illustrates and thereby fixes a truth or experience as a picture fixes a face or landscape in the mind.[6]

When Christ says, "Salt is good; but if the salt have lost his saltness, wherewith will ye season it? Have salt in yourselves, and have peace one with another," no one accuses Him of a *non sequitur*. The parable is obviously a parallelism, the illumination of the unknown by its exact consonance with a truth previously perceived. There is no attempt to argue from an observation about salt to an injunction about peace, which is the kind of argument Mr. Evans and other critics accuse Chesterton of attempting. Yet they never so accuse Christ: not merely, it may be suspected, because it is patently not the job of Divinity to argue. One reason Christ is sacrosanct is probably to be found in a popular tradition that

He is solemn: as if He had never produced the wine for a feast. If Christ had playfully turned the lost sheep of the parable of the ninety and nine into a stray from a herd of kangaroos, it would have been all up with Him as a theologian. Apropos of solemnity Chesterton observes:

If you say that two sheep added to two sheep make four sheep, your audience will accept it patiently—like sheep. But if you say it of two monkeys, or two kangaroos, or two sea-green griffins, people will refuse to believe that two and two make four. They seem to imagine that you have made up the arithmetic, just as you have made up the illustration of the arithmetic. And though they would actually know that what you say is sense, if they thought about it sensibly, they cannot believe that anything decorated by an incidental joke can be sensible.[7]

The joke and the parable are not so far apart as they seem; for properly speaking even the statement, "two sheep and two sheep make four sheep" is a parable; a common corporeal phenomenon corresponding exactly to the unfamiliar, almost mystical idea that two and two make four. Sheep as a parallel to an abstract idea are fascinating and fantastic enough to make one wonder why the solemn critic should boggle at kangaroos. It is still more important, however, to recognize the almost irresponsible fantasy by which the word "two," either as a set of wriggly marks on paper or as a man-made noise at once abrupt and cooing, is made to correspond to that same abstract idea, the idea of twoness. The word is certainly not the reality; it is only something analogous to the reality. Apropos of allegorical painting, Chesterton asks:

But what does the word "hope" represent? It represents only a broken instantaneous glimpse of something that is immeasurably older and wilder than language, that is immeasurably older and wilder than man: a mystery to saints and a reality to wolves. To suppose that such a thing is dealt with by the word "hope," any more than America is represented by a distant view of Cape Horn, would indeed be ridiculous. It is not merely true that the word itself is, like any other word, arbitrary; that it might as well be "pig" or "parasol"; but it is true that the philosophical meaning of the word, in the conscious mind of man, is merely a part of something immensely larger in the unconscious mind, that the gusty light of language only falls for a moment on a fragment, and that obviously a semi-detached, unfinished fragment of a certain definite pattern on the dark tapestries of reality. It is vain and worse than vain to declaim against the allegoric for the very word "hope" is an allegory and the very word "allegory" is an allegory.[8]

Language is not thought, and thought is not reality, any more than figures in a ledger are money, or money is human wealth. Yet one must always use language and thought, as the book-keeper must always use figures and coins. One can never, in short, escape parallelism; and we never speak but in parables.

"I doubt whether any truth can be told except in parable," Chesterton makes one of his characters say; and the proposition is accompanied by its Chestertonian corollary: "I doubt whether any of our actions is really anything but an allegory."[9] That these observations were self-evident to him in the light of his metaphysical intuition of being may be guessed from the central lines of the poem *Ubi Ecclesia*:

> Where things are not what they seem,
> But what they mean.[10]

One who saw the world as a vast inter-reflecting organism saw language implicated in that reality along with every other ingredient. When Chesterton writes, in short, the very words he uses are part of the vision he exploits; his facility in word and image derives from a real analogical relation, of which he was keenly aware, between language and the other parts of reality. To tax him with verbalism is to deny the existence of analogy, to deny that anything is like any other thing, to deny therefore that connecting things by thinking has any metaphysical meaning: all that. It is rank nominalism.

He was a sturdy realist; and his vision of things showed him very clearly what he could most readily do. His favorite logical device was the *reductio ad absurdum*, because that line of argument springs most readily, with the least possible degree of abstractness, from a direct metaphysical perception. When you see that something is absurd, you are in touch with reality.

It is true for the same reason, though insufficient, to say that he was more concerned with stating cases than proving them. It is still more accurate to say that he strove above all else to *show* men what he saw, on the principle that a thing once seen is its own proof.

> False religion . . . is always trying to express concrete facts as abstract; it calls sex affinity; it calls wine alcohol; it calls brute starvation the economic problem. The test of true religion is that its energy drives exactly the other way; it is always trying to make men feel truths as facts; always trying to make abstract things as plain and solid as concrete things; always trying to make men, not merely admit the truth, but see, smell, handle, hear, and devour the truth.[11]

Hence Chesterton's purple patches, his parallelisms, his vivid word-play. Hence his perpetual reiteration of concrete imagery, concrete argument: his avoidance of language which unhappily no longer keenly indicates reality, having been abstracted to death. In *Orthodoxy* he says

> If you say, "The social utility of the indeterminate sentence is recognized by all criminologists as a part of our sociological evolution towards a more humane and

scientific view of punishment," you can go on talking
like that for hours with hardly a movement of the grey
matter inside your skull. But if you say, "I wish Jones
to go to gaol and Brown to say when Jones shall come
out," you will discover, with a thrill of horror, that you
are obliged to think. The long words are not the hard
words, it is the short words that are hard. There is
much more metaphysical subtlety in the word "damn"
than in the word "degeneration."[12]

On these principles, in the kind of argument we
have caught Mr. Evans deploring, Chesterton trans-
lates the jargon of a Swiss professor about the conscience into short words which force men to think,
and then reproduces the pattern of absurdity presented by those naked words with a corresponding
pattern secured by putting for the word "conscience"
the word "nose." He does not argue, he need not
argue, that the statement about conscience is as
absurd as the statement about noses. It was always
absurd. One does not even need to know the meaning of the word "conscience" to see the absurdity.
The law of logic has been transgressed, and it is a
logical, not a factual, flaw that is being exposed. Unfortunately, logic is a strangely unfamiliar tool:
equally unfortunately, no one has ever seen a conscience, though all men have seen noses. Hence it
is that nonsense talked about the conscience has a
fair chance of passing muster, though corresponding
talk about noses fairly shrieks its own falsity.

Having grasped all this, the reader of the following passage will not accuse Chesterton of irresponsible play:

The first argument is that man has no conscience because some men are quite mad, and therefore not particularly conscientious. The second argument is that man has no conscience because some men are more conscientious than others. And the third is that man has no conscience because conscientious men in different countries and quite different circumstances often do very different things. Professor Forel applies these arguments eloquently to the question of human consciences; and I really cannot see why I should not apply them to the question of human noses. Man has no nose because now and then a man has no nose—I believe Sir William Davenant, the poet, had none. Man has no nose because some noses are longer than others, or can smell better than others. Man has no nose because not only are noses of different shapes, but (oh, piercing sword of scepticism!) some men use their noses and find the smell of incense nice, while some use their noses and find it nasty. Science therefore declares that man is normally noseless; and will take this for granted in the next four or five hundred pages, and will treat all the alleged noses of history as the quaint legends of a credulous age.[13]

The nose-pattern repeating the conscience-pattern is the type of all Chesterton's writing. The truths with which he deals are not those of a rarefied kind which the normal mind can only discover at the further end of a wearisome logical process; they are mostly elementary truisms which have only to be *seen.* "It is the paradox of human language," he says of the fundamental convictions, "that though these truths are in a manner past all parallel hard and clear, yet any attempt to talk about them always has the appearance of being hazy and elusive.[14] The best that language can do is indicate them, and the best language for the purpose is that which indicates most sharply. It follows that Chesterton's concern throughout his writing will be to frame paragraphs which first, correspond with the reality whereon he has fixed his eye, and second, shout for attention. "We try," he says, "to make our sermons and speeches more or less amusing, . . . for the very simple and even modest reason that we do not see why the audience should listen unless it is more or less amused."[15]

Chesterton's humility here underrates his achievement. We have discussed in Chapter III the rhetorical function served by much of his paradox; equally important is the way word, image, and epigram cooperate to do superbly something that could not otherwise be done at all, when, as too rarely, he disciplines them rigidly in the service of metaphysical statement. The example of the nose and the conscience cited above is really excessively simple; as an instance of the precision and flexibility Chesterton was capable of when he chose, it is worth while examining the working of the paragraph, already quoted on page 76, which develops the comparison between the mystical mind and the dandy's dressing-room. As usual, he opens with a specific example, the wooden post:

> When (our contemporary mystics) said that a wooden post was wonderful, they meant that they could make something wonderful out of it by thinking about it. "Dream; there is no truth," said Mr. Yeats, "but in your heart."

The quotation from Yeats recalls to the reader any number of similar statements, and so places Chesterton's simplification in relation to the entire tradition he is attacking. With the next sentence the controlling image is introduced:

> The modern mystic looked for the post, not outside in the garden, but inside, in the mirror of his own mind. But the mind of the mystic, like a dandy's dressing-room, was entirely made of mirrors. That glass repeated glass like doors opening inwards for ever; till one could hardly see that inmost chamber of unreality where the post made its last appearance.

The word "dandy" reflects on "mystic" as much as on "dressing-room"; and at the same time the stock image of the mirror of the mind is subtly transmuted into a vivid, pejorative image of a room lined with mirrors. "Dressing-room" brings to mind the triptych mirrors at tailors', where everyone has had experience of infinite multiple reflections; and the additional comparison of doors opening inwards

for ever gives additional concrete force to the idea.
In the final clause, "inmost chamber of unreality"
gives new precision to the comparison of the mystic's
mind to a room: and the sequence ends where it
began, at a deeper level of penetration. In the next
sentence, mirrors return, with a difference:

And as the mirrors of the modern mystic's mind are
most of them curved and many of them cracked, the
post in its ultimate reflection looked like all sorts of
things . . . etc.

It is perhaps unnecessary to point out that
"cracked," applied to the mirror and to the mind,
has double force. Another functional pun turns up
immediately afterwards:

But I was never interested in mirrors; that is, I was
never interested in my own reflection—or reflections.

"Reflection" is of course supplied by the mirror-
imagery, with an overtone of vanity vs. humility;
Chesterton is never far from the moral implications
of metaphysics. And the pun introduced by "reflections" brilliantly refocuses the entire enquiry on
the operations of the mind, preparing for a statement of the positive conclusions:

I am interested in wooden posts, which do startle me
like miracles. I am interested in the post that stands
waiting outside my door, to hit me over the head, like
a giant's club in a fairy tale.

The giant's club recalls the episode of bumping into a post which was the initial stimulus of the essay; but it here functions locally as a physical image of the metaphysical surprise evoked in "posts which do startle me like miracles." In the next sentence the door outside which the post stands introduces a transition to the doors of the senses which open on that mental room with which the preceding passage has been concerned: and the peroration after so much preparation carries enormous force:

All my mental doors open outwards into a world I have not made. My last door of liberty opens upon a world of sun and solid things, of objective adventures. The post in the garden; the thing I could neither create nor expect; strong plain daylight on stiff upstanding wood; it is the Lord's doing and it is marvellous in our eyes.

Careful study along these lines of the way in which the transition from image to image is made in similar passages will reinforce the constant theme of this chapter: that Chesterton's writing at its best is concerned with fixing exactly a statement of a metaphysical vision, by indicating relationships of word and example within that vision. He is not inventing illustrations, he is perceiving them. The conventional patristic divine, Jeremy Taylor, summarizes the kind of analogical perception that this writing is exploring:

Thus when (God) made the beauteous frame of heaven and earth, he rejoyced in it, and glorified himself, because it was a glasse in which he beheld his wisdom, and Almighty power: . . . For if God is glorified in the Sunne and Moon, in the rare fabric of the honeycombs, in the discipline of Bees, in the œconomy of Pismires, in the little houses of birds, in the curiosity of an eye, God being pleased to delight in those little images and reflexes of himself from those pretty mirrours, which like a crevice in a wall thorow a narrow perspective transmit the species of a vast excellency: much rather shall God be pleased to behold himself in the glasses of our obedience. . . .[16]

Gerard Manley Hopkins puts it more succinctly: "This world then is word, expression, news of God."[17] Chesterton would interpret that news. Perception of this fact reduces to a simple manifestation of humility his claim to be a journalist rather than an artist.[18] If he was not a creative artist, he was, when he took the pains, an extremely competent workman, framing intricate analogies to interpret the supreme analogy which he saw all around him. He was in this sense an artist because he was the highest kind of journalist, having as his object truth.

He suggests in *William Blake* the way in which the analogist's art must be called in to present truth:

In the modern intellectual world we can see flags of many colours, deeds of manifold interest; the one thing we cannot see is the map. We cannot see the simplified statement which tells us what is the origin of all the trouble. How shall we manage to state in an obvious and alphabetical manner the ultimate query, the primordial point on which the whole modern argument turns? It cannot be done in long rationalistic words; they convey by their very sound the suggestion of something subtle. One must try to think of something in the way of a plain street metaphor or an obvious analogy. For the thing is not too hard for human speech; it is actually too obvious for human speech.[19]

The plain street metaphor or the obvious analogy are for Chesterton the simple key to the problem of conveying reality, short-circuiting as they do the fore-doomed attempt to trace the contradictory labyrinth of being with any continuous rational thread. "Long rationalistic words . . . convey by their very sound the suggestion of something subtle"; and being is the reverse of subtle. It is simple, though the principle of analogy shows it to be paradoxically complicated as well. A locomotive is both simple in essence and complicated in detail; one would scarcely call a locomotive subtle. And one should beware of trying to describe a locomotive to the uninitiated by rationalistically describing its workings, beginning with the vaporization of heated water, lest its puffing power come to seem very subtle indeed. One does better to call it an iron horse.

No one who has finally grasped these points will press the question, why Chesterton's prose is so intricate. Too wise to try to explain the obvious, he drew pictures of it; and his pictures, like those of

God with whom the artist is often audaciously compared, took on life; a life of their own; a life of alliteration and epigram, of sudden unexpected correspondences, of accidental patterns writhing and weaving with all the crawling energy of the Gothic architecture which was his craftsman's ideal.[20]

We have shown in analysing the mirror-passage how Chesterton in his best work manipulates his images functionally, to control the reader's response towards a total meaning which cannot itself be briefly and exactly stated. We have stated further Chesterton's explicit view that brief and exact statement of an analogical reality is in fact *a priori* impossible. These principles may be tidied up in a new statement of the ubiquitous necessity of paradox: for in paradox is the practitioner of art, even expository art, perpetually landed. The reason is that the thing, the work of art, that he is constructing must both hang together itself and be consistent with the reality on which his eye is fixed. Insofar as it hangs together itself, insofar as it obeys its own artistic laws, it will have being, which is analogical. Its statements, to put it another way, will in only a relative sense be logically interdependent. Insofar as it is consistent with that other being whose shadow it is, it will not only tend to be twisted out of coherent shape, but it will partake of the paradoxicality of its prototype. The law that all being is intrinsically analogical operates

Wake, concealed as it is by the use of some dozen different languages, is simply to fold paradoxes back upon themselves in such a way as to utter both contrasting halves simultaneously. When Joyce writes "phoenish," he is telescoping alpha and omega, the end and the beginning, *finish* and *phoenix*. When he writes, "For nought that is has bane," he says simultaneously, "Nothing that exists is evil," and "The appearances of evil have no permanence; they were not and they shall not be"; simultaneously posing and resolving the problem of pain.

The oddly esoteric vocabulary of *Finnegans Wake* represents a final straining attempt to overcome the basic paradox of art and make the Thing identical, beyond any possibility of separation, with its verbal vehicle. It utterly defeats paraphrase. It is not a little startling to see how this audacious, almost blasphemous attempt to re-utter the world-generating Word, to achieve a totality corresponding to the totality which is of God, achieves its object—insofar as it does achieve it—by virtue of multi-layered paradoxes whereby a river is all rivers, riverdom, woman, all of life, and but half of life; and a stone is an innkeeper, a dreamer, the fount of life, quite dead, and both food and feeder at his own funeral feast.

Joyce, as we shall see, has other affinities with Chesterton as a myth-maker. It is surely a demonstration of the contemporary critical muddle to find the most advanced experimenter of his time building upon the same first principles, and exploiting the same kind of analogical perception, as the man whom avant-garde critics decry as the very type of hearty Toryism.

Indeed it is the analogical perception which makes it possible for *Finnegans Wake* to be taken seriously; though Joyce, who, it is true, offers far more temptation to the inept than does Chesterton, has suffered from essentially the same charge of verbalism. Chesterton's insistence that the artist keep his eye on the object finds in the career of Joyce a particularly ironic vindication.

We have shown that Chesterton's eye never wandered from the object, from an especially intricate simultaneous perception. It is helpful to remember that he elevated this principle into a positive prescription. It is, to begin with, scarcely necessary to point out that keeping one's eye on the object does not mean copying the externals of the object. Rather it means knowing what the object is, knowing from the inside. This interior knowledge when it can be obtained is a guarantee against the errors introduced by falsely-framed concepts. The surest way to find out that the "economic man" doesn't exist is to try to draw a picture of him. It was the attempt to draw pictures of things that existed only as concepts that

vitiated the later poetry of Blake; it took his art into
that unreal otherworld of doubts and riddles that
has for the past thirty years been the playground of
a certain kind of critic. On the failure of Blake
Chesterton commented,

> No pure mystic ever loved pure mystery. The mystic
> does not bring doubts and riddles: the doubts and
> riddles exist already. . . . The mystic is not the man who
> makes mysteries, but the man who destroys them. The
> mystic is one who offers an explanation which may be
> true or false but is *always* comprehensible. The man
> whose meaning remains mysterious fails, I think, as a
> mystic.[21]

The early Blake, he says, like every great mystic,
was also a great rationalist.[22] In this sense, another
great rationalist is Chesterton's own Father Brown.
It is startling to count the Father Brown stories
which turn on the war of reason with mystification.
Father Brown, the professional supernaturalist, is
constantly at war with the sham supernatural. In
"The Arrow of Heaven" there is talk of a curse,
misdirecting attention from a simple stabbing. In
"The Perishing of the Pendragons" a family doom
and a supernaturally flaming tower are reduced to
mere arson and shipwreck. In "The Doom of the
Darnaways" an ancient interdiction boils down to
a very modern murder-plot.[23] These stories are repeated parables of the true function of the artist and
seer; their wildly paradoxical solutions are true; the

straightforward, frequently supernatural explanation is falsification. The cloak of evil, Chesterton
seems to be saying, is the false paradox; the trap
of truth is the incomplete paradox.

Equally the trap of truth is the word written in
the void, the writer's eye not firmly fixed on the
object. A parable of this principle is presented in
the contrasting peasants of the following passage:

> Knowing nine hundred words is not always more
> important than knowing what some of them mean. It
> is strictly and soberly true that any peasant, in a mud
> cabin in County Clare, when he names his child
> Michael, may really have a sense of the presence that
> smote down Satan, the arms and plumage of the paladin
> of paradise. I doubt whether it is so overwhelmingly
> probable that any clerk in any villa on Clapham Com-
> mon, when he names his son John, has a vision of the
> holy eagle of the Apocalypse, or even of the mystical
> cup of the disciple whom Jesus loved. In the face of
> that simple fact, I have no doubt about which is the
> more educated man; and even a knowledge of the
> *Daily Mail* does not redress the balance. It is often said,
> and possibly truly, that the peasant named Michael
> cannot write his own name. But it is quite equally true
> that the clerk named John cannot read his own name.
> He cannot read it because it is in a foreign language,
> and he has never been made to realize what it stands for.
> He does not know that John means John, as the other
> man does know that Michael means Michael.[24]

Chesterton's acute awareness of this danger was
one of the things that led him to prefer journalism

to a more cloistered if less distracting life among the "pure artists." For it is patently true that for one such genius as Eliot, "the most conscious point in his age," there are a hundred poseurs of Bloomsbury with their eyes turned inward upon their egos. In exoneration of his trade he wrote,

A poet writing his name upon a score of little pages in the silence of his study may or may not have an intellectual right to despise the journalist: but I greatly doubt whether he would not morally be the better if he saw the great lights burning on through darkness into dawn, and heard the roar of the printing wheels weaving the destinies of another day. Here at least is a school of labour and of some rough humility, the largest work ever published anonymously since the great Christian cathedrals.[25]

He preferred journalism because it kept him constantly in touch with real work and real problems. What troubled him about the efforts of the emptier modern artists was that they had their eyes on no object: they meant nothing. The heresy of Realism, which celebrates things for what they seem and not for what they mean, he presents under the parable of a gigantic Gothic cathedral revisited by a priest who has lost his memory:

He saw piled in front of him frogs and elephants, monkeys and giraffes, toadstools and sharks, all the ugly things of the universe which he had collected to do honour to God. But he forgot why he had collected them. He could not remember the design or the object.

He piled them all wildly into one heap fifty feet high; and when he had done it all the rich and influential went into a passion of applause and cried, "This is real art! This is Realism! This is things as they really are!" . . .

The finest lengths of the Elgin marbles consist of splendid horses going to the temple of a virgin. Christianity, with its gargoyles and grotesques, really amounted to saying this: that a donkey could go before all the horses in the world when it was really going to the temple. Realism means a lost donkey going nowhere.[26]

He closes this essay "On Gargoyles" with an illuminating reference to his own work:

These monsters are meant for the gargoyles of a definite cathedral. I have to carve the gargoyles, because I can carve nothing else; I leave to others the angels and the arches and the spires. But I am very sure of the style of the architecture and of the consecration of the church.[27]

Journalist or no, gargoyle-carver or no, he nevertheless knew what his words meant, and the contradictions into which language leads; he knew what being meant, and the contradictions implicit in it; and he did not shrink from the baffling task of making the latter visible through the former.

Keeping in mind all the criteria we have considered: Chesterton's insistence that art be responsible to truth and rooted in the perceptions of the artist; the scope and explicitness of Chesterton's metaphysical perception, within which he moved so freely; yet disabling both, his patent incapacity to realize particular conflicts seriously enough to produce significant poetry: keeping all this in mind, what are we to make of his output of novels and stories? What kind of relevance have they to his lifelong moral and metaphysical concern?

The novel that is not simply documentation owes its vitality to the epigram at its heart: it works by expansion.

Chesterton's novels expand his elsewhere concisely developed perceptions, function in the same way, and have the same kind of value: but with (as Belloc said of the scriptural parable) a story to capture the interest of the reader. The reader who has followed the analysis above of the richly allusive passage on the mirrors of the mystic's mind, with its shifts of imagery and expanding and contracting symbolism, can see that the movement of ideas is exactly like that of a Chestertonian story; and the experienced reader can readily imagine the story Chesterton might have made of it. The reader familiar with the Father Brown collection will know the story he did make of it: *The Man in the Passage*.

Like a paragraph of vintage Chestertonian exposition, the Chestertonian novel or story constructs a web of analogies. Its value is ultimately moral: the value of any parable. His novels, like his poems, are the products of a born philosopher, not of a born dramatist. The Father Brown stories, for example, with all their machinery of murder and repentence, and all the genuine moral interest in the fact of human sin that makes them unique among detective stories, are patently devoid of the intense dramatic life of *Crime and Punishment*. This is not to say that they exist, like the ordinary mechanical detective story, only as neat constructions: rather they exist as ingenious analogues of psychological facts. Chesterton knew perfectly well, and repeatedly asserted, that as human documents they are trifling; he took them seriously enough to write them because they reflect, like everything else he wrote, the unique metaphysical intuition it has been the purpose of this book to explore.

To say that the characters exist as abstractions, that the life of the stories is conferred entirely by the continual local brilliance of the writing, and that they function ultimately as expansions of the philosophic conflicts in his paragraphs of moral and metaphysical paradoxes, is to say that Chesterton's fiction is not drama but parable; on a large scale, as in *The Man Who Was Thursday*, it is allegory: myth. It is unnecessary to recall the tradition of Christian allegory in which they are rooted: *Pilgrim's Progress* may be cited as a late example, springing from the tradition that had flowered in the morality plays. It is more fruitful and suggestive to point to two men whose perceptions tended to be, like Chesterton's, of a detached and philosophical kind, and much of whose output is explicitly on the level of myth: William Blake and James Joyce.

Much of the recent re-emphasis on Blake is based on the appetite of a collapsing civilization for sustaining myths, and to a current belief that the artist fulfilling his supreme function assumes a sort of priestly character and becomes myth-maker. That the myth tends to become dehumanized is counted no demerit by the modern taste for the abstract. At best, the myth-maker erects a pantheon and brings it to life; and so bringing the universe to life, he presents that life under the figure of something living: a man: hence the approach of the most ambitious philosophical speculation to the ancient conception of the macrocosm: the gigantic man who is all things. This conception is everywhere present in Christian thought: to say that in Adam all die and in Christ all are made alive is literally to think in terms of the fall of one all-subsuming human form and the redemption effected by an all-sustaining human God.

Men capable of thinking with any comfort in terms of such magnitude have been few; one is William Blake, another is James Joyce; a third is Gilbert Chesterton. Blake in the nineteenth century and Joyce in the twentieth represented the pattern of the cosmos by the figure of a gigantic man, or by the eternal recurrence of a gigantic circle or wheel; or contemplating the persistence of the unfallen state as an eternal reality lying behind the fallen, by both together.

Such figures were Chesterton's, and they were the logical fruit of his talent for metaphysical perception dramatized on a large scale. One of his themes, developed in *The Man Who Was Thursday*, is the figure of fallen and scattered men conceived as parts broken off the whole and perfect man, free according to their limited being to recapture some analogical image of that former wholeness by pushing to the limit such virtues as now lie within their powers: an image of the isolation of soul from soul. It is in this sense that he sees the supernatural goodness of saint after saint arising to union with God and yet intrinsically imperfect because its emphasis is on goodness of one kind. It is in obedience to this principle that "St. Francis, in praising all good, could be a more shouting optimist than Walt Whitman; St. Jerome, in denouncing all evil, could paint the world blacker than Schopenhauer."[28] Saints may contradict one another's virtues and be right, because saints live in a fallen world. The best man develops only a corner of his potential virtue; he is but a fragment of the unfallen Adam.

Following from and completing this idea is the

corollary conception of good men everywhere seemingly at odds, breaking each other's heads in the name of good, yet ultimately fighting all on the same side, the warring members of the cosmic man.

At the end of *The Napoleon of Notting Hill* there stands a passage pushing this idea to the utmost of which Chesterton was capable, a passage pointing back to the celestial wars of Blake and forward to the cosmic paradoxes, as yet unuttered, of Joyce. There comes out of the silence and darkness that followed the settling of the dust upon the last battlefield of Notting Hill a chill voice saying:

"So ends the Empire of Notting Hill. As it began in blood, so it ended in blood, and all things are always the same."

And another voice replies out of the ruins,

"If all things are always the same, it is because all things are always heroic. If all things are always the same, it is because they are always new. To each man one soul only is given; to each soul only is given a little power—the power at some moments to outgrow and swallow up the stars. If age after age that power comes upon men, whatever gives it to them is great. . . . We who do the old things are fed by nature with a perpetual infancy. No man who is in love thinks that anyone has been in love before. No woman who has a child thinks that there have been such things as children. . . . Yes, oh, dark voice, the world is always the same, for it is always unexpected."

. . . Wherein the experienced reader will hear the soft Irish voice of James Joyce: "Teems of times and happy returns. The seim anew." Then the first voice retorts again that all is dust and nothingness, and again the second voice carries forward its theme:

"Men live, as I say, rejoicing from age to age in something fresher than progress—in the fact that with every baby a new sun and a new moon are made. If our ancient humanity were a single man, it might perhaps be that he would break down under the memory of so many loyalties, under the burden of so many diverse heroisms, under the load and terror of all the goodness of men. But it has pleased God so to isolate the individual human soul that it can only learn of all other souls by hearsay, and to each one goodness and happiness come with the youth and violence of lightning, as momentary and as pure. And the doom of failure that lies on all human systems does not in fact affect them any more than the worms of an inevitable grave affect a children's game in the meadow. Notting Hill has fallen; Notting Hill has died. But that is not the tremendous issue. Notting Hill has lived."

But the first voice laughs on, scoffing at Notting Hill as vanity. Then they know one another: Auberon Quin, who gave Notting Hill its charter for a joke, and Adam Wayne, who fought for that charter as a creed. And Wayne finishes:

"The equal and eternal human being will alter (our) antagonism, for the human being sees no antagonism between laughter and respect, the human being, the common man, whom mere geniuses like you and me can only worship like a god. When dark and dreary days come, you and I are necessary, the pure fanatic, the pure satirist. We have between us remedied a great wrong. We have lifted the modern cities into that poetry which everyone who knows mankind knows to be immeasurably more common than the commonplace. But in healthy people there is no war between us. We are but the two lobes in the brain of a ploughman. Laughter and love are everywhere. The cathedrals, built in the ages that loved God, are full of blasphemous grotesques. The mother laughs continually at the child, the lover laughs continually at the lover, the wife at the husband, the friend at the friend. . . . Let us go out together. . . . Let us start our wanderings over the world. For we are its two essentials. Come, it is already day."[29]

That, as the conclusion and summation of his earliest novel, shows clearly the abstract and mythological conception on which it is based. The "equal and eternal human being" was to become Sunday, the fantastic anarchist whose face in the last wild chase of *The Man Who Was Thursday* is concealed from sight, and who turns out finally to be the chief of police: Sunday, "huge, boisterous, full of vanity, dancing with a hundred legs, bright with the glare of the sun, and at first, somewhat regardless of us and our desires;" Sunday—"Nature as distinct from God."[30]

The reconciliation of that antagonism between him who scoffs and him who worships is accomplished in *The Man Who Was Thursday*; for the antagonist of them both turns out to be the leader of them both. He is like the cosmic man of so much quasi-mystical speculation: the stupendous figure through whose limbs circle the stars. In him is transcended the isolation of soul from soul, which begets both loneliness and its blood-brother courage. The cosmos has the pattern of a man, which is one of its two traditional ultimate patterns; the other being the wheel, the unending cycle, the serpent with its tail in its mouth, which Chesterton also perceived and abominated, summing it up through countless scattered passages in the restless, formless patterns of Turkish carpets, the restless, pointless cycle of Nirvana, and the annihilistic self-contemplation of the East.[31] The cosmos has become a man, a man of will and energy and fantastic beauty, a man and therefore a cross.[32] And when, in the final sentences of *The Man Who Was Thursday*, the last mask is torn off the face of Nature, there is displayed the older face of God: "Can ye drink of the cup that I drink of?"

The restless brother-battle consequent on the Fall and resolved in a transcendental resurrection was a myth that Chesterton arrived at early in life: saw, embodied in a hasty novel subtitled "A Nightmare," and passed over. He said, with acute self-penetration, that he was a journalist because he could not help being a controversialist, and hence never a novelist.[33] Had he been a novelist he might well have lingered with that single vision, and elaborated it as it deserved to be elaborated, for his largest talents lay towards myth and allegory, and that vision, or rather the perception underlying that vision, underlay everything that he was later to write, in however scattered or fragmentary a form. Only twice in English letters has that vision been perceived and elaborated towards its perfection: in the Apocalyptic vision of *Jerusalem* and in that other nightmare of the dreamer of *Finnegans Wake*. Sunday is the gigantic Albion of Blake, the nameless panheroic HCE of Joyce. The Two Voices disputing amid the failing firelight of Notting Hill are the rebellious Orc and the sunlit Los of Chesterton's great predecessor, the scoffing Shem and the conserving Shaun of his great contemporary. Had he given himself to his art as did these men, he might have been received into their trilogy. It was as well that he did not. Myths tend to be sterile; Blake's reputation, after the flurry of symbolic interpretation has died down, will probably rest on his early dramatic lyrics, and Joyce's on the inevitable discovery that his myth is vitalized by an intense personal conflict. That Chesterton's potentiality, had he chosen to be an artist, lay in the direction not of drama but of myth, is another way of saying that with his secure metaphysical perception he would have found his true fulfilment as a great philosopher. The times, how-

NOTES

Pending the compilation of such a Chesterton anthology as is projected in the Introduction, these notes are offered as assistance to the scholar and as a guide to further reading. Since there are generally speaking no standard editions of Chesterton's works, it would have been useless to attempt a scholarly uniformity; I have merely cited the editions I had handy, of which a list is appended.

The reader will find that the argument of this book is buttressed chiefly by four works: *Heretics* (1905), *Orthodoxy* (1908), *St. Thomas Aquinas* (1933), and the *Autobiography* (1936). These books, from the beginning and end of Chesterton's career, demonstrate the remarkable consistency of his perceptions, which, as I have continually insisted, deepened but never shifted. They also contain on the whole his freshest statements of first principles, the first pair reflecting initial enthusiasm and the second pair confident maturity. The most enthusiastic Chestertonian cannot but notice many signs of fatigue in the reiterated restatements of the middle years. *William Blake,* like most of Chesterton's criticism, is far more about Chesterton than about his subject; it contains valuable hints on difficulties of perception and communication. *The Everlasting Man* (1925), being less given than some later works to detailed doctrinal defense, is his most ambitious demonstration of the rooting of the history of human activity in psychological reality, and the most valuable single record of the place of the Incarnation in his thinking.

The really valuable works about Chesterton are two: Maisie Ward's *Gilbert Keith Chesterton*, and Hilaire Belloc's *On the Place of Chesterton in English Letters*. The first, intended as the definitive biography, is an infinitely useful source-book for hundreds of quotations, letters, and comments elsewhere unpublished. Belloc's fragment is whole, right, and penetrating; but Belloc's advanced age, his natural reticence, and his adherence to the classical prescription that a thing conceived as a brief appreciation should not admit expository digressions, make it more of a handrail than a searchlight.

Those who have properly digested Chesterton will find that most of the other available books and articles are explaining the obvious. Maurice Evans' *G.K. Chesterton* (Cambridge University Press, 1939) is here and there penetrating but, because starting from false first principles, continually erroneous. *G.K. Chesterton—A Criticism*, written and published anonymously in 1908 by his brother Cecil, is a marvel of insight and prophecy but contains little that will be new to the reader of Chesterton's output during the following twenty-eight years.

LIST OF EDITIONS CITED

Saint Thomas Aquinas, Sheed and Ward, New York, 1933.
The Poet and the Lunatics, Cassell, London, 1929
Heretics, John Lane, London, 1905.
The Well and the Shallows, Sheed and Ward, London, 1937
　　(The Ark Library).
Orthodoxy, John Lane, London, 1908.
The Everlasting Man, Hodder & Stoughton, London, 1925.
William Blake, Duckworth, London, 1910.
Tremendous Trifles, Methuen, London, 1909.
The Coloured Lands, Sheed and Ward, New York, 1938.
The Uses of Diversity, Methuen, London, 1920.
Christendom in Dublin, Sheed and Ward, London, 1932.
Autobiography, Hutchinson, London, 1936.

Robert Browning, Macmillan, London, 1903.

George Frederick Watts, Duckworth, London, 1902.

The Napoleon of Notting Hill (in *A G.K. Chesterton Omnibus*), Methuen, London, 1936.

Alarms and Discursions, Dodd Mead, New York, 1911.

Collected Poems, Methuen, London, 1933.

Introduction to the Book of Job, Cecil Palmer & Hayward, London, 1916.

The Judgement of Dr. Johnson, Sheed and Ward, London, 1927.

St. Francis of Assisi, Hodder & Stoughton, London, 1923.

All Things Considered, Methuen, London, 1908.

What's Wrong with the World, Cassell, London, 1910.

The Ball and the Cross, Wells Gardner, Darton & Co., London, 1910.

Fancies Versus Fads, Methuen, London, 1923.

The Man Who Was Thursday, Arrowsmith, Bristol, 1908.

The Incredulity of Father Brown, Cassell, London, 1911.

The Wisdom of Father Brown, Cassell, London, 1914.

Irish Impressions, Collins, London, 1919.

The Innocence of Father Brown, Cassell, London, 1911.

The following four critical works are also cited:

Maisie Ward, *Gilbert Keith Chesterton,* Sheed and Ward, New York, 1943. (Cited as "Ward.")

Maurice Evans, *G.K. Chesterton,* Cambridge University Press, 1939. (Cited as "Evans.")

Hilaire Belloc, *On the Place of Chesterton in English Letters,* Sheed and Ward, New York, 1940. (Cited as "Belloc.")

Cecil Chesterton, *G.K. Chesterton,—A Criticism,* Alston Rivers, London, 1908. (published anonymously.)

I: PRELIMINARY

1. See Ward, p. 619. After rapidly dictating about half the book, he flipped through some authorities and

dictated the remainder without looking at them again. Maisie Ward also quotes Prof. Etienne Gilson's statement that Chesterton had guessed everything the serious scholars were wrestling towards.

2. *St. Thomas Aquinas,* p. 206.
3. *The Poet and the Lunatics,* p. 128.
4. Quoted in Ward, p. 66.
5. "To St. Michael in Time of Peace." Published posthumously by G.K.'s Weekly, Sept. 24, 1936, pp. 42-43.
6. *Heretics,* p. 109.
7. Evans, p. 1. His opening sentence is, "The works of Chesterton are essentially a product of their age," and he feels that "to the end he was refuting forgotten heresies."

II: PARADOX AND ITS NECESSITY

1. Belloc, p. 21.
2. B. Ifor Evans, *A Short History of English Literature,* Pelican Books, 1940, p. 213.
3. Legouis and Cazamian, *A History of English Literature,* J. M. Dent, London, 1937, p. 1305.
4. Quoted in Ward, p. 155.
5. Ibid, p. 586.
6. Ibid, p. 587.
7. In the essay, "Where is the Paradox?", *The Well and the Shallows,* p. 269.
8. *Orthodoxy,* p. 15.
9. *Heretics,* p. 129.
10. Ibid, p. 82.
11. Ibid, p. 129.
12. *The Everlasting Man,* p. 195.
13. Lancelot Andrewes, *Sermons,* Oxford, 1841, vol. I p. 92.
14. *William Blake,* p. 58.
15. "On Evil Euphemisms," in *Come to Think of It.*
16. *Heretics,* p. 65. See also "The Advantages of Having One Leg" in *Tremendous Trifles,* pp. 37 sq., and

"Wonder and the Wooden Post" in *The Coloured Lands*, pp. 157 sq.

17. "Quando igitur res sunt mensura et regula intellectus, veritas consistit in hoc quod intellectus adaequatur rei, ut in nobis accidit." *Summa Theologica*, I. q. 21. 2.c.

18. *Heretics*, p.47.

19. Ibid, p. 109.

III: THE IDEA OF ANALOGY

1. For a concise treatment of analogy, see the Rev. Gerald B. Phelan, *Saint Thomas and Analogy*, Marquette University Press, Milwaukee, 1941.

2. *Heretics*, p. 82.

3. Serpent Reasonings us entice
   Of Good & Evil, Virtue & Vice. . . .
   Blind in Fire with shield & spear,
   Two Horn'd Reasoning, Cloven Fiction,
   In Doubt, which is Self contradiction,
   A dark Hermaphrodite We stood,
   Rational Truth, Root of Evil & Good.
   Poetry and Prose of William Blake 1 vol. ed. Geoffrey Keynes, Nonesuch Press, London, ed. 4, 1939, pp. 577-578. The poem is part of the cycle entitled "For the Sexes: The Gates of Paradise." Other remarks on Reason, less immediately comprehensible because of Blake's inversion of the roles of Jehovah and Satan, are to be found in "The Marriage of Heaven and Hell" (Keynes, pp. 181 sq.) and elsewhere. Urizen, Blake's bound, tyrannous Prince of the Natural World, is identified with Reason, who in his fallen form becomes the "idiot questioner".

4. Phelan, op. cit., p. 2.

5. Ibid, p. 25. "Of course the ultimate basis upon which such analogies rest is the proportion existing between the essence (*quod est*) and the existence (*esse*) of every being that is; from which it follows that every meta-

physical perfection, every metaphysical concept, and every metaphysical term, is of its very nature analogical. This is indeed a very far-reaching statement, for it implies that whenever one uses such a common word as "is" or "true" or "good," or any other term express- ing a metaphysical or transcendental object of thought, the meaning of that word never remains exactly the same, but is always proportionate to the nature of the being of which it is said."

From this conclusion it is not hard to understand the necessity of paradox in trying to tell the truth about something.

6. *William Blake,* p. 177.

7. Plenty of essays are built around this rapture. On lamp-posts and omnibuses, see "Lamp-Posts" in *The Uses of Diversity*, p. 7. See also "What I Found in My Pockets" (*Tremendous Trifles,* p. 87); "Wonder and the Wooden Post" (*The Coloured Lands,* p. 157), etc.

8. *St. Thomas Aquinas,* pp. 207-211.

9. *The Uses of Diversity,* p. 7.

10. *Christendom in Dublin,* p. 25. Cf. *Orthodoxy,* p. 69: "Art is limitation; the essence of every picture is the frame."

11. Quoted in Ward, p. 61.

12. Ibid, p. 62.

13. *Autobiography,* pp. 331-338.

14. Ibid, p. 338.

15. *Jerusalem,* plate 15, lines 12-20 (Keynes, p. 449).

16. *Heretics,* p. 65.

17. Thomas Traherne, "The Salutation."

18. Crashaw, "Saint Mary Magdelene, or The Weeper," from *Carmen Deo Nostro* (1646).

19. *Writings of Tertullian,* Clark, Edinburgh, 1870, vol. 2 p. 234.

20. Spenser, *Faerie Queene,* Bk. I, Canto 1, Stanza viii.

21. James Joyce, *Ulysses,* Random House, New York, 1934, p. 766.

22. Browning, "Childe Roland to the Dark Tower Came," stanza xii.
23. *Robert Browning*, p. 159.
24. Maisie Ward, introduction to *The Coloured Lands*, p. 15.
25. *Orthodoxy*, pp. 15-16.
26. "Auguries of Innocence," lines 1-4 (Keynes, p. 118).

IV: THE WORD

1. Cf. *Collected Poems*, p. 326: "Ecclesiastes":
     There is one sin; to call a green leaf grey,
     Whereat the sun in heaven shuddereth.
   This poem appeared in the *Wild Knight* volume in 1900, when Chesterton was twenty-six years old.
2. *The Picture of Dorian Gray*, ch. 1.
3. *William Blake*, p. 177.
4. See especially the introductory chapter to *The Everlasting Man*, the avowed strategy of which is to paint Christianity at its strangest: "When its fundamentals are doubted, as at present, we must try to recover the candour and wonder of the child; the unspoilt realism and objectivity of innocence. Or if we cannot do that, we must try at least to shake off the cloud of mere custom and see the thing as new, if only by seeing it as unnatural." p. 15.
5. *The Well and the Shallows*, p .14. The quotation comes from the introductory "Apology for Buffoons," which should be read in its entirety.
6. For Companionate Marriage, see above, Ch. II, note 15. The second remark is quoted by Evans, p. 136.
7. *Heretics*, p. 21.
8. Ibid, pp. 48-49.
9. *Christendom in Dublin*, p. 39.
10. *William Blake*, p. 80.
11. *Heretics*, p. 137.
12. Ibid, p. 153.

13. *William Blake*, p. 94.
14. Ibid, p. 178.
15. Ibid, p. 58.
16. *Tremendous Trifles*, p. 31.
17. Belloc, pp. 71-72. See also p. 32.
18. op. cit., vol. I, p. 386.
19. Andrewes, op. cit., vol. IV, pp. 394-5.
20. See on this point Jacques Maritain's treatment of the theory of the sign, in *Ransoming the Time*.
21. T. S. Eliot, *Ash-Wednesday;* Gertrude Stein, *Four Saints in Three Acts;* James Joyce, *Portrait of the Artist as a Young Man.*
22. *Orthodoxy*, p. 51.
23. *George Frederick Watts*, p. 134.
24. From an extensive collection of Renaissance para-doxes I take the following at random: In 1579 the Stationers' Register licensed a "Paradox proving by reason and example that baldness is much better than bushy hair;" Horace has a discourse in praise of hair and attacking baldness in *Satiromastix* (1602); Crispinus speaks a paradox in praise of baldness (ibid); Leonard Wright's *Display of Dutie* (1616) contains a section "In prayse of baldnesse"; Nashe refers to a paradox in defense of short hair.
    The relationship between these and the Chesterton passage is patently fortuitous; but that he should have indulged, without apparent awareness of his prede-cessors, in a standard Renaissance mode of paradoxical display is at least a psychological curiosity.
25. Belloc, p. 34.

V: THE WORLD

1. *The Well and the Shallows*, p. 15.
2. Ibid, p. 10.
3. *St. Thomas Aquinas*, p. 199 and ch. vi-vii, passim.
4. *Orthodoxy*, p. 56.

5. Ibid, loc. cit.

6. Ibid, p. 59.

7. Ibid, loc. cit.

8. Ibid, p. 61.

9. Ibid, p. 62.

10. Ibid, pp. 66-67.

11. Ibid, p. 63.

12. Cf. *Orthodoxy*, pp. 46 sq.: "Mysticism keeps men sane," etc. The word is similarly misused throughout *William Blake*.

13. Cf. Max Plowman's remark: "Blake is sometimes ignorantly regarded as a person of hazy 'mystical' ideas who had no use for reason and was therefore proudly unreasonable. The contrary is the truth. Because he was able to think with great clarity he saw the limits of logic and put reason in the hierarchy of intelligence where every good thinker has put it, under the guidance of poetry. . . . Only those capable of using reason in a high degree will be able fully to appreciate his consistent reasonableness." Plowman, *Introduction to the Study of Blake*, J. M. Dent, London, 1927, p. 63.

14. *St. Thomas Aquinas*, p. 210.

15. *Alice in Wonderland*, ch. i.

16. *William Blake*, p. 138.

17. *St. Thomas Aquinas*, p. 208

18. *Orthodoxy*, p. 46.

19. Cf. *Heretics*, p. 82; *St. Thomas Aquinas*, p. 210.

20. *Orthodoxy*, pp. 46-48.

21. Quoted in Cecil Chesterton's *G. K. Chesterton—A Criticism*, p. 113.

22. Ibid, loc. cit.

23. *St. Thomas Aquinas*, pp. 179-180.

24. *The Coloured Lands*, p. 108.

25. *Autobiography*, pp. 133 sq.

26. Ibid, p. 137.

27. *Heretics*, pp. 139-140.

28. *The Napoleon of Notting Hill,* p. 13.
29. Ibid, p. 14.
30. *Tremendous Trifles,* p. 69.
31. Ibid, p. 220.
32. Adam Wayne in *The Napoleon of Notting Hill,* Innocent Smith in *Manalive,* Patrick Dalroy in *The Flying Inn,* are three of them. The curious reader may like to reckon up the red-haired heroines.
33. *The Napoleon of Notting Hill,* pp. 91-92.
34. Ibid, pp. 172-173.
35. Ibid, p. 174.
36. *Tremendous Trifles,* p. 89.
37. *Alarms and Discursions,* pp. 30-31.
38. *Orthodoxy,* p. 105.
39. *Tremendous Trifles,* p. 91.
40. *Collected Poems,* p. 204.
41. *The Coloured Lands,* pp. 159-161.
42. *Orthodoxy,* pp. 80-81.
43. *Autobiography,* p. 150.
44. *St. Thomas Aquinas,* p. 206.
45. *Autobiography,* p. 330.
46. Ibid, pp. 331-332.
47. *G. K. Chesterton—A Criticism,* pp. 116-117.
48. Ibid, loc. cit. Quoted by Cecil from G. K.'s controversy with Blatchford.
49. *Introduction to the Book of Job,* pp. xxi-xxii.
50. Ibid, p. xix.
51. *Collected Poems,* p. 284.
52. *William Blake,* p. 142.
53. *Christendom in Dublin,* p. 16.
54. *Heretics,* p. 110.
55. *Collected Poems,* p. 144.
56. Ibid, p. 82.
57. Ibid, p. 141.
58. See note 48 above.
59. *The Everlasting Man,* p. 230.

60. *St. Thomas Aquinas*, pp. 139-140.
61. *The Everlasting Man*, Part II, ch. 1: "The God in the Cave."
62. Ibid, pp. 195-197.
63. *The Napoleon of Notting Hill*, passim.
64. *Tremendous Trifles*, pp. 145-151; Ward, pp. 260-262; *Autobiography*, pp. 31 sq.
65. Cf. *Orthodoxy*, pp. 112-114, where regarding the universe as small rather than large is presented as a necessary preliminary to praise and called "a sort of sacred thrift."
66. *The Everlasting Man*, p. 198.
67. *William Blake*, p. 210.
68. *Collected Poems*, p. 307.
69. Ibid, p. 72.
70. Evans, p. 157.
71. *The Everlasting Man*, p. 200.
72. Ibid, p. 210.
73. *The Judgement of Dr. Johnson*, p. 38.
74. On Man as a contingent being, cf. *St. Francis of Assisi*, ch. 5; and *The Poet and the Lunatics*, p. 27, where it is fancied that St. Peter, being crucified upside down, "Saw the landscape as it really is; with the stars like flowers, and the clouds like hills, and all men hanging on the mercy of God."
75. Quoted in Chesterton's obituary notice in *The New York Times*, June 15, 1936.
76. *All Things Considered*, pp. 13-14.
77. *Heretics*, pp. 63-65.
78. Ibid, p. 67.
79. Ibid, p. 151.
80. *Introduction to the Book of Job*, p. xxvii.
81. Ibid, p. xxii.
82. *Christendom in Dublin*, p. 20. Cf. *What's Wrong with the World*, passim.
83. *The Coloured Lands*, pp. 233 sq.

84. *Manalive*, Part II, ch. iii.
85. *The Ball and the Cross*, ch. xii.
86. *Orthodoxy*, ch. i.
87. *The Everlasting Man*, p. 9.
88. *Fancies Versus Fads*, p. 8.
89. Ibid, pp. 219 ff.
90. *Tremendous Trifles*, p. 203.
91. *Orthodoxy*, pp. 170-172. See the whole chapter, "The Paradoxes of Christianity," pp. 146-185.
92. Cf. *Fancies Versus Fads*, p. 120: "The brotherhood of man, being a spiritual thing, is not concerned merely with the truth that all men will die, but with the truth that all men know it."
93. Cf. *The Everlasting Man*, pp. 240-247.
94. *William Blake*, p. 179. The idea occurs even earlier; it is in *Orthodoxy*, pp. 254-255; *Robert Browning*, pp. 178-179; and the final pages of *The Man Who Was Thursday*.
95. *The Ball and the Cross*, p. 279.
96. *G. K.'s Weekly*, Sept. 24, 1936, pp. 42-43.

VI: THE WORD AND THE WORLD

1. *Gloria in Profundis* (chorus from an unfinished play), Faber and Faber, London, 1927. Not included in any collection.
2. T. S. Eliot, *Four Quartets*, Faber and Faber, London, 1944, p. 21.
3. Andre Malraux, "Is Europe Dead?," *New Leader*, Jan. 18, 1947, p. 11.
4. *Heretics*, p. 33.
5. Evans, pp. 147-149.
6. Belloc, pp. 36-40.
7. *Autobiography*, p. 169.
8. *George Frederick Watts*, pp. 94-95
9. *The Poet and the Lunatics*, p. 130. Cf. *George Frederick Watts*, p. 122, which at an early stage of Chester-

ton's realization mentions tentatively "the existence of genuine correspondences between art and moral beauty, the existence, that is to say, of genuine allegories."

10. *Ubi Ecclesia,* Faber and Faber, London, 1929. Not included in any collection.

11. *Alarms and Discursions,* p. 59.

12. *Orthodoxy,* p. 229.

13. *The Uses of Diversity,* pp. 93-94.

14. *Fancies Versus Fads,* p. 43.

15. *The Well and the Shallows,* p. 18.

16. Quoted in *Gerard Manley Hopkins,* by The Kenyon Critics, New Directions, New York, 1945, p. 19.

17. Quoted by G. F. Lahey, S. J., *Life of Gerard Manley Hopkins,* p. 124.

18. *Autobiography.* p. 288.

19. *William Blake,* The entire passage (pp. 196 sq.) repays study.

20. Cf. *Alarms and Discursions,* pp. 14-15.

21. *William Blake,* p. 131.

22. Ibid, p. 83.

23. *The Incredulity of Father Brown,* pp. 31-70; *The Wisdom of Father Brown,* pp. 185-215; *The Incredulity of Father Brown,* pp. 225-265.

24. *Irish Impressions,* pp. 52-53.

25. "A Word for the Mere Journalist." *Darlington North Star,* Feb. 3, 1902. Quoted in Ward, p. 156.

26. *Alarms and Discursions,* p. 14.

27. Ibid, p. 15.

28. *Orthodoxy,* p. 167.

29. *The Napoleon of Notting Hill,* Bk. V, ch. iii, pp. 193-200.

30. Quoted in Ward, p. 193, from an interview given by Chesterton to explain certain phases of the book, nearly twenty years after it was written.

31. Cf. *St. Thomas Aquinas,* pp. 135-136: "He who will not climb the mountain of Christ falls into the abyss

of Buddha. . . . Most other alternatives of heathen humanity . . . are sucked back into that whirlpool of recurrence which all the ancients knew"; *The Everlasting Man*, Bk. II, ch. v, where "The Wheel of Asia" is taken as the antithesis of Christianity; also the story, "The Wrong Shape," in *The Innocence of Father Brown*, where the priest-detective says of the crooked knife, " 'It's the wrong shape in the abstract. Don't you ever feel that about Eastern Art? The colours are intoxicatingly lovely; but the shapes are mean and bad—deliberately mean and bad. I have seen wicked things in a Turkey carpet. . . . They are letters and symbols in a language I do not know; but I know they stand for evil words. . . . The lines grow wrong on purpose—like serpents doubling to escape.' "

32. *The Man Who Was Thursday*, p. 329.
33. *Autobiography*, p. 289.

PUBLISHER'S NOTE

Since Mr. Kenner prepared his study in Canada, the editions listed in his bibliography are largely English. United States editions also have been brought out by the following publishers: Dodd, Mead & Company: *The Ball and the Cross, Collected Poems, The Everlasting Man, Fads Versus Fancies, The Father Brown Omnibus* (including "The Innocence of Father Brown," "The Incredulity of Father Brown," "The Wisdom of Father Brown"), *Heretics, Irish Impressions, The Man Who Was Thursday, Orthodoxy, The Poet and the Lunatics, Tremendous Trifles, The Uses of Diversity, What's Wrong with the World,* and *G. K. Chesterton—A Criticism,* by Cecil Chesterton; Doubleday, Doran and Company: *St. Francis of Assisi;* E. P. Dutton & Co., Inc.: *William Blake;* The Macmillan Company: *Robert Browning;* Sheed & Ward, Inc.: *The Autobiography of Gilbert Keith Chesterton, What's Wrong with the World* (in the Catholic Masterpiece Tutorial Series), *The Well and the Shallows.*